JEWISH FOR GENTILES:

A HANDBOOK FOR SURVIVAL
IN OUR ASSIMILATED SOCIETY

By

Toby R. Serrouya

To Greg,

who I hope will enjoy
this book and find it an
excellent source of reference

John Serrouya

ISBN: 1-4107-3840-X (e-book)
ISBN: 1-4107-3839-6 (Paperback)

Library of Congress Control Number: 2003092187

This book is printed on acid free paper.

Printed in the United States of America
Bloomington, IN

1stBooks – rev. 04/10/03

Dedicated in loving memory to my son, Alan, who always wanted to do the right thing and have those who he knew and loved do the right thing as well.

PROLOGUE

Growing up Jewish in the Bronx, New York in the 1950s and the 1960s I thought that the whole world was Jewish. There was, in truth, a lot of "us" and a few of "them". By some strange twist of fate our entire Jewish neighborhood had in its midst a prestigious Catholic all boys school known as All Hollows. One side of the school was attached to our apartment building and we viewed it as "forbidden" territory. We would peer wistfully through the black iron bars that were inserted into a huge archway that stood between us and the most perfectly square gigantic playground we had ever seen.

While we had the brick walls that fronted the myriad of apartment buildings that made up our neighborhood, the city streets and a sporadic handful of parks in which to play – they had this tantalizing playground.

In the evenings, we would often walk around the corner to a small park like opening, which provided easy access for us into the playground. The fathers who taught at the school and lived on the premises always seemed to turn a friendly cheek the other way. We would play squash, slug and stickball as our parents watched us from outside. At evening's end we would disappear back into our world. They, the boys who attended kindergarten through twelfth grades, and who inhabited the hallways and classrooms of the school, would return in the morning to claim what was rightfully theirs. At the time, it seemed to all of us like an excellent working arrangement. There were times when we would pass one another in the street and even look at one another and smile timidly, but throughout all of my childhood years I could never recall an instance when "we" and "they" merged into "us". This would only occur once we grew up, educated ourselves, moved out of our protective and restrictive neighborhood existence and began to follow our dreams; our professions; our spouses; our destinies.

Today we find ourselves living in a world where our neighborhood, school, work and leisure time pursuits have led to the merger of "we" and "they" into "us". Working closely with and coming to know people from various religious and ethnic and racial backgrounds, we often take for granted that our new acquaintances and friends know all about our own customs and traditions. This cannot be further from the truth. It became apparent to me when I recently experienced the sudden death of my twenty-seven year old son. Upon my return to work, while being welcomed back, the one theme that resonated from my non-Jewish colleagues was that upon learning of the death of my son, they had all wanted to do the right thing according to Jewish-law, but were not quite certain what the right thing was! We talked at length about this. Two colleagues in particular, Kathleen Dylewski, and Maureen Senius, encouraged me to write this book by giving me a title for this book as a starting point and by meeting with me in order to highlight and out line which specific areas they felt a need to learn about. This reference book was born out of a tragic circumstance in my life. I hope that you will learn from it and find it especially useful when the need arises to turn unfamiliar situations into comfortable experiences. But most importantly, I hope that you will only have to refer to it for happy occasions.

ACKNOWLEDGMENTS

I want to thank Rabbi Saul Zucker, Rosh Mesivta, of The Mesivta of North Jersey for the time and diligence that he spent in lending his Talmudic knowledge to the editing of this manuscript for accuracy of Orthodox Jewish law. He reviewed the legal aspects of this text; however, as Jewish Law is complex, a competent rabbinic authority should be consulted for any questions. I know that for him this was truly a labor of love due to the relationship he had with my son. Nevertheless, his involvement in this project has made it possible for me to present a far more accurate and appropriate piece of work to my readers.

I also want to thank my husband, Elyse, for all the patience, understanding, encouragement and love that he gave to me which helped me to survive an event so tragic that I had initially believed it to be non-survivable!

I want to thank my eighty-eight year old Mother for not only being able to provide me with all the ingredients and necessary steps to be taken in the preparation of the recipes found in this book, but for also providing me with all the ingredients and necessary steps to be taken in order for me to be able to make a smooth transition from the world of my childhood to the world that I now live in.

Last, but certainly not least, I want to thank my loving cat, Menachem (named for Menachem Begin who was one of Israel's Prime Ministers), for exercising great restraint and not chewing through the computer wires, and not swatting at the computer keyboard as I typed. But most important of all, I want to thank him for not snoring each time that he fell asleep on the couch in our office as I worked on this project.

TABLE OF CONTENTS

CHAPTER ONE: Love and Courtship

Love and courtship Jewish-style can appear to be the ordinary and familiar ritual recognizable to most of us, or unique and unfamiliar. This depends upon which branch of Judaism one or both of the couple were brought up in and have committed themselves to remain an integral part of for the rest of their lives. Men and women who make up the traditional branch of Judaism are commonly known as orthodox or observant Jews and will almost always select their mate from amongst their own group. The followers of Orthodox Judaism believe that God gave both the Written and Oral Law to Moses on Mount Sinai. For the Orthodox Jew only a literal observance of Torah and the subsequent Codes of Law is adequate. The word Torah can refer to the laws on a particular subject, or to all of the law. The word Torah is most often used when referring to the teaching of G-d to the Jews.

ORTHODOX JEWS

Orthodox Jews often get to know one another socially through school, neighborhood, in their synagogues or through their youth group affiliations. As a group, you will find that members who embrace the Orthodox ideology will follow the Sabbath (or Shabbas) strictly in the sense that all work stops from sundown on Friday evening through sundown on Saturday evening. They will not do anything of a work-related nature including the use of electricity of any kind (timers can be found in all Orthodox Jewish homes so that the lights can be set to go on and off at appropriate times). All food must be cooked and prepared before the Sabbath begins. There is no listening to the radio, or watching of television even if the most important game of the World Series might happen to fall on the Sabbath. Orthodox Jews will not drive, receive or initiate telephone calls or conduct business on the Sabbath. On that day, there will be no exchange of money and no one will even carry money with them, credit cards included. You will never see a man with a wallet or a woman with a pocketbook in any Orthodox Jewish community on the Sabbath.

There are of course exceptions. A member of the medical profession is permitted and indeed expected to do whatever is needed to attend to the welfare of their patients, even if it involves breaking one or several laws of keeping the Sabbath. If someone is injured or stricken with the type of illness that requires immediate medical attention then the main objective quickly becomes to get that person to a doctor or hospital as quickly as possible. When the infamous 1973 Yom Kippur War broke out during the most holy day of the Jewish Year, and Israel found itself confronted with its own destruction by the surrounding Arab countries, the entire country ran out of their synagogues and immediately swung into a state of high alert and activity to prepare to send their divisions off to battle. Young men who had been engaged in solemn prayer and fasting found themselves within a mere twenty-four hours transformed into part of a superb fighting force that would lead to their eventual victory. This never could have happened if the decision was made to continue the observance of the holiday until sundown as Jewish law dictates. If they had remained in prayer and in their synagogues the probability was great that they would have been left with only their synagogues and no country!

The sudden outbreak of war and medical emergencies aside, there is a firm commitment on the part of Orthodox Jews that during their lifetime they will strictly adhere to the laws set down in the Torah. This seems to be most easily and sensibly done by choosing a partner who has been raised and molded in this same environment. Once love is declared, the courtship period is quite short. In many cases hand holding and touching of any sort only begins after the couple have announced their engagement. Intimacy only begins after marriage. The young couple will often register for gifts, and may or may not have an engagement party.

THE ENGAGEMENT PARTY GIFTS AND ESPECIALLY UNDERSTANDING THIS NUMBER "18" THING

If you find yourself invited to an engagement party or wish to send an engagement gift, the gift selection can be found amongst the typical array of house ware, silver and china listed in a registry, or you can always send or give money. If you are going with money, this will be your first opportunity to think in terms of eighteen. The number eighteen has great significance for the Jewish people. The Hebrew word for eighteen is "chai" and it means life. The number eighteen is highlighted in the recital of the AMIDAH which is a prayer consisting of eighteen blessings which is recited at each of the three daily synagogue services. This prayer is always said standing. The number eighteen is woven throughout the core and fabric of the day. It is therefore a natural progression that it has come to play a part in gift giving. Depending upon your financial circumstances and close ties and feelings to the bride and groom to be, your gift can be given in multiples of eighteen. Thus, gifts in the amounts of $18, $36, $54, $72, etc. are frequently given and recognizable at all forms of celebrations. Of course, you can get as creative as you wish with the number 18. Please think only in terms of addition or multiplication. Thus, $18 can easily become $180 or $1800, or $360.

KOSHER GIFT GIVING

If you wish to bring a gift that is food related, the word kosher must begin to flash in front of you like a broken neon sign. The Hebrew word Kashrut refers to the body of laws governing food. The original lists of forbidden species in the Bible were explained as follows: (1) Animals fit for consumption must both chew the cud and have a cloven hoof (such as sheep and cows) (2) Birds of prey are forbidden (3) Fish may only be eaten if they have both fins and scales (4) Animals must be slaughtered in a particular way and the meat must then be salted and washed to remove all traces of blood (5) Meat foods and milk foods may not be eaten or even prepared together. With this in mind see how well Biblical scribes have prepared you to walk into any upscale department store and shop for your engagement gift.

THE "INFAMOUS" FORBIDDEN FOODS

Remembering that the young couple who is planning to have a kosher home will not be eating shrimp or lobster, do not give in to an outrageous sale and allow yourself to purchase a set of shrimp cocktail glasses. Remember not to select the lovely lobster forks or butter knives for the meat pattern they have selected. I once received shrimp cocktail glasses as an engagement gift and keeping a kosher home, have spent the past thirty years trying to have them be useful. With some trial and error I have been able to recreate them as my strawberries with vanilla ice cream parfait glassware. If you have decided to help the young couple complete their selected china and silverware patterns, do not think that a computer error has been made because two patterns are listed.

NOW I UNDERSTAND THIS NUMBER "2" THING

Here is the time to be introduced to the number two. For a couple who will be keeping a kosher home after marriage, think in terms of two because anything kitchen related will be needed twice. Think dairy-related meals and meat-related meals. There will be two sets of dishes, two sets of silverware, two sets of pots and pans, two sets of dishtowels, and we are not even going to touch on Passover yet! This can be a good thing for you as the purchaser. In this case, there is far less worry about duplicating. When the gift opening time of the engagement party arrives, you do not have to get that sinking feeling when you witness the bride to be excitedly opening a present of a cake plate eerily similar to the one you have spent a lot of time and thought shopping. Smile smugly, relax, have another sandwich and think two! Those surrounding you will be doing the same.

GIFTS WITH RELIGIOUS UNDERTONES

While browsing through the gift department section you should seek out the large selection of religious items made by Lenox. Their beautiful challah tray, which is used to hold bread over which a prayer will be made on the Sabbath and festivals, or the bread-cutting knife, makes a presentable and useful gift. One of my favorite selections for gift giving is a Kiddush cup. Any reputable department store will have a gift department with an adequate selection of silver plated, sterling silver or silver Kiddush cups. This gift will be used often in the homes of orthodox, conservative and reform couples. The Kiddush cup is filled with wine and is held by the man while reciting the prayer, known as Kiddush, to sanctify Sabbaths or festivals. It is forbidden to eat on a Sabbath or festival until after the Kiddush has been recited. So whenever you find yourself invited to a Sabbath or holiday meal, always remember to keep your eyes on that Kiddush cup and never dig into the gefilte fish, chopped liver, or salad until it is placed safely on the table! Quickly after this ritual has been completed a short prayer will then be recited as the bread is being cut and passed out to all of the people who will partake in the meal. By the time you get your piece of bread you will be safely able to enjoy eating the first course to be served. Do not forget that the bottle of wine will also always need a decorative wine coaster to sit on.

THE SOURCE FOR EVERYTHING JEWISH

An excellent source for gifts with a slight or heavy religious overtone to them is a place that I like to refer to as my one stop-shopping trip. It is basically run as a mail order house and is called *The Source for Everything Jewish*. They publish gift catalogues four times a year and to order one, simply call their toll free number at 1-800-426-2567. Upon receiving their catalogue you will soon find appropriate gifts for any occasion that run the gamut from engagement gifts, wedding gifts, house gifts, holiday gifts, baby gifts, all the way to Bar and Bat mitzvah gifts. You will find a varied and interesting selection of gifts in the areas of chinaware, silverware, toys, food, clothing, all different types of artwork, books, CDs, videos, games and jewelry. The price ranges are just as varied. These gifts will range in price anywhere from $12.95 for a "sports *kippah*" (each *kippah* having been designed out of either suede or leather, and made to resemble either a basket ball, a foot ball, a soccer ball or a base ball) and will go up in price to $950 for a diamond and menorah ruby star pendant which is 14K gold and comes with a 14K gold chain. The gift can be either sent to you or gift wrapped and sent on to your friend. Of course, like with any catalogue order, there is an additional charge for shipping and handling. This is such a great catalogue that I have often sent the catalogue to friends who have expressed their frustrations in selecting a *Hanukkah* gift for a very special couple they know who happens to be Orthodox.

The courtship period for Orthodox Jewish couples is not a lengthy one. Due to the fact that the wedding is often planned within a short time frame, you may find yourself attending a middle of the week wedding, very often on a Thursday evening. As soon as you learn of an impending engagement and marriage, check your vacation day and personal day availability. You might want to allow yourself the time to leave early on the day of the wedding and not come into work on the day following the wedding. These weddings last well into the night and are a lot of fun!

CONSERVATIVE JEWS

When love strikes people who embrace the Conservative Jewish ideology, the courtship period can be of a longer duration. Conservative Judaism is a religious movement within Judaism, which arose, in the mid-nineteenth century. People who follow Conservative Judaism believe in the validity of the traditional forms and precepts of the religion, but with some moderation. How do I know if these people are Conservative Jews? (you may be asking yourself). Stop asking yourself and ask them. It is not considered a prying or rude question, and for your purposes, a necessary one. If you get an affirmative answer go on to bring up the question of this kosher thing.

Many Conservative Jews will keep a kosher home so this knowledge is a must in terms of all food – related purchases.

THE ABCs OF KOSHER WINE

If you are one of those who is into thinking of the ultimate combination of cute, useful and delicious all wrapped into one gift (i.e. a case of wine with personalized labels for the future bride and groom from that outrageously expensive and yuppie winery in California) – think again! Unless the wine is kosher, it will not be appreciated or used. Do not despair because today there are significant selections of kosher wines in liquor stores. Gone are the days when kosher wine was a synonym for sweet wine that came in a large bottle with a twist off cap. I was well into my thirties and dating my husband when I discovered that all wine did not have a twist off cap. That discovery came on a cold, winter weekend while preparing my first dinner for him. Knowing of his French background, I had bought a bottle of wine to accompany our dinner. When I went to open it, to my horror I discovered that the cap was stuck in the bottle! Thinking I had purchased a defective bottle of wine, I went flying back to the liquor store with bottle in hand where a bewildered, but benevolent store owner proceeded to introduce me to the world of the corkscrew. He showed me how it worked and let me practice using it. In hindsight, I think of how truly kind he was and how often he must have told this story! Today, if you do not see the type of kosher wine you are looking for, simply ask for it and if not in stock, any liquor store can place an order for you. You can get anything from Zinfandel, Merlot, Cabernet Sauvignon, and Chardonay to Champagne. And yes, you can still purchase that sweet wine with the twist off cap! You can have your wines, but alas, not with those adorable labels! Of course, you can again get creative (think computer generated labels) because you now have experience in tapping into your creativity resources by having mastered that number eighteen thing.

At this point you may be wondering what to do if you wish to purchase Scotch, Rye, or Bourbon. Because we are not dealing with the "grape" issue (the grape being the ingredient used in the preparation of all wines and which must be prepared in a specific way to be considered a "kosher grape") please feel free to purchase any type of hard liquor you want and it will be acceptable as a kosher gift.

REFORM JEWS

The third branch of Judaism, which makes up the largest group of practicing Jews in this country, is known as Reform Judaism. It was created as an attempt to make Judaism more relevant by introducing new prayers in the vernacular and abbreviating the traditional prayers found in the prayer book. In recent years American Reform Judaism has become more traditional and many people today do not find that big a difference between Reform Jews and Conservative Jews. One big, obvious difference and an important one to note for your purposes, is that Reform Jews often do not keep kosher homes or keep kosher when outside their home. With this group you might very well be introduced to the concept of a kosher-style home.

THE KOSHER-STYLE HOME

If the couple you are engagement gift shopping for is planning to set up a kosher-style kitchen in their home, stop thinking in terms of two. Start thinking in terms of no mixing of dairy with meat products while a particular meal is being prepared and served. There will be one set of dishes and one set of silverware. In addition, start thinking in terms of no forbidden foods such as bacon or lobster or pork or shrimp being brought into the home. Do know that the meats, cheeses, wines, etc. that are to be found in such a home will not necessarily be strictly kosher. You may be able to order those great wines with the personalized labels, but do check before the order is placed.

DOES EVERY HILTON HAVE A SYNAGOGUE?

You will soon discover that no matter which ideology of Judaism your friends follow, their wedding plans are already underway. They have already selected a date, and have reserved a catering hall or synagogue. America's synagogues have been built with hosting large and impressive weddings in mind. Thus, if you find yourself invited to a synagogue wedding, please know that both the ceremony and the wedding reception will be taking place at this one location. The same thing holds true for a wedding to be held in a catering establishment. At all Jewish weddings the rule of thumb is that both the religious ceremony and the festive wedding reception are held at the same facility, be it a synagogue or a catering establishment.

THINK MODESTY AND NO TOUCHING!

Finally, someone's family Rabbi has already been contacted. You will indeed be told far in advance of the date selected, and to keep it free. So just sit back and wait for that invitation to arrive and then make your preparations to attend your friend's wedding. Shop for that new dress, but if you have been invited to an orthodox Jewish wedding please remember that the word modesty is key to appropriate dress amongst orthodox Jewish women and men alike. As difficult as it might be to walk away from that sensational low cut, sleeveless dress that you have dieted yourself down to be able to fit into – exert great control and do so! In the long run you will save yourself and your hosts and surrounding guests from an uncomfortable situation. Men should buy that new suit or look into tuxedo rentals since "black tie" or "black tie optional" is frequently seen on wedding invitations. One more thing – start to think about that wedding gift!

CHAPTER TWO: Here Comes the Bride

NEVER ON A SATURDAY (AFTERNOON)

A Jewish wedding is always mixed with strong doses of traditionalism. It is a fact that no matter which ideology of Judaism the bride and groom follow; you are in for a learning experience. Jewish weddings are held most often on a Saturday or Sunday evening or on a Sunday afternoon. But do not forget the possibly of mid-week weddings. A wedding can never be held on the Sabbath. In the Jewish religion, as you have already learned, the Sabbath begins with nightfall on Friday evening and concludes with nightfall on Saturday evening. Thus, no Jewish wedding ceremony will ever be held on a Saturday morning or afternoon. If you find yourself invited to a Saturday wedding, it will only begin after sundown. Needless to say, weddings held in the wintertime will have a much earlier starting time then those weddings held in the summertime. No matter what time of the day or day of the week the ceremony and accompanying rituals will always be the same, depending upon which branch of Judaism the families of the bride and groom have embraced.

THE POPE WEARS THAT!

If you have been invited to an Orthodox Jewish wedding, start thinking in terms of the word separate and never stop thinking of the word kosher which means among other things, separation of meat and dairy products. If you are being served a meat meal, that meal will never be accompanied by any dairy products. So if you are one of those who insists on fresh milk or real thick cream when your White Russian is being made, think again! No milk! The cocktail hour will be held first. When you arrive you will be struck by three things. Number one is that there is no gift table. The guests have all either sent their gifts from reputable and hopefully upscale Department Stores or are planning to give money at the end of the wedding reception. Secondly, all the men guests are actually wearing those little hats that the men were given upon entering. They are in the color scheme of the wedding and have an imprinted saying on the inside, which will bear the names of the bride and groom in both English, and in Hebrew and their wedding date. As you begin to stare more intensely at these little hats you do recognize them as being oddly similar to what the Pope always wears on his head. That little hat or skullcap is known as a *yarmulke* (the Yiddish word) or a *kipah* (the Hebrew word). Orthodox Jewish men wear these skullcaps all the time because it is presumed that during a great part of the day one will be engaged in some sort of prayer or prayers and it is a sign of great humility and respect to God Almighty to have your head covered while engaged in prayer and while uttering God's name.

Thirdly, you will be struck by how pale the groom looks. This is not just a bad case of nerves or a stomach virus. Both he and the bride have been fasting all day, as is Jewish tradition, and will not eat until after the ceremony when the time comes for him and his bride to be alone for the first time. So whatever you do, do not greet him by telling him that you have just the thing to qualm his nerves and proceed to shove a delicious meatball or a stuffed mushroom into his mouth and then go to the bar and return quickly with a double scotch. The groom will at some point disappear from the room. He is not being rude or running away from you. At this time you and all the guests will be ushered toward a part of the room, or into another room, where the bride is sitting with her mother and future mother-in-law on either side of her.

THE ORTHDOX "WEDDING UNVEILING CEREMONY"

Just as you are acclimating yourself to this visual, you begin to hear loud singing coming from behind you. As you turn, you see the groom being carried into the room on the shoulders of a group of men. These men are made up of his friends and family members. The music and chanting is pulsating and captivating. As this group comes closer and closer to the bride it soon becomes apparent that the groom is being spearheaded directly toward the bride's face where he begins to pick up her veil and look at the bride and then put the veil down.

This is done a couple of times. The premise behind this ceremony is to enable the groom to be certain that the woman who he intends to marry is indeed the woman dressed as a bride with the veil over her face. Once this is done, the groom with his all-male escorts disappears out of the room singing, just as they had arrived. It is now time for the wedding ceremony to begin, so if you have not yet checked out the carving stations, do so now because you will never see them again! At the same time, say goodbye to your spouse or date or whomever of the opposite sex you have been visiting with, because it will be a while before you see them again!

As you walk toward the room where the ceremony will take place, you begin to experience a warm inner feeling knowing that you did the right thing by writing a check to the bride and groom as a wedding present. If you followed the old eighteen rule that is great. If you did it the more familiar way in multiples of twenty-five, still great! All is well and your heart goes out to those friends who are still awkwardly either carrying or looking for a place to deposit their wrapped gifts. You had told them, you had warned them, but alas, they simply could not imagine a wedding taking place in America without a gift table!

SEPARATE SEATING

If the ceremony is being held in a synagogue, you will enter the sanctuary. If it is being held in a hall you will enter a beautiful room decorated and set up as a sanctuary. Upon entering, it will become immediately evident to you that the men are being ushered to one side of the aisle, while the women are being ushered to the other side of the aisle. Amongst orthodox Jews, it is believed that while engaged in prayers and rituals, it is of utmost important to focus on prayer and God. The opposite sex, who from day one has been considered a major distraction, are therefore segregated so that there will be no such distraction during the course of this particular ceremony.

THE WEDDING CEREMONY

The modern Jewish marriage ceremony is really a combination of two separate acts that bring together the concept of betrothal or engagement, and the concept of consummation of the marriage. The two parts have been combined from the Middle Ages on. Once the marriage contract known as the *Ketubah* is agreed upon, the bridegroom is led to the bride under the marriage canopy known as the *Huppah*. This symbolizes the marriage chamber. You will see that the *Huppah* is open at the sides and can be made of anything from a simple prayer shawl to an elaborate array of flowers. In most cases you will find yourself looking at more flowers than you have seen since your fourth grade class trip to either the Bronx or Brooklyn Botanical Gardens. In a Jewish marriage ceremony you will witness the presentation by the groom to the bride of an item of monetary value (usually a ring) of nominal worth. It has evolved that during the wedding ceremony an inexpensive wedding band is placed on the bride's finger. Only after the ceremony and before the wedding reception does the bride place upon her finger the more expensive wedding band that she will wear from that day on. The second act refers to cohabitation or consummation of the marriage. The married couple symbolically carries this out when they seclude themselves after the ceremony for a short period of time in a private room adjacent to the area where the ceremony took place. At that time they will break their fast and hopefully loose their sickly pale coloring.

The wedding party is made up of the traditional cast members: a best man, a maid and/or matron of honor, ushers, bridesmaids, cute little flower girls, a squirmy ring bearer and the beaming grandparents and parents. One difference you will observe is that the groom walks down the aisle accompanied by both of his parents. The concept behind this being that both of his parents were with him at his birth and have raised him and have nurtured him spiritually and in every other way to bring him to this point as he walks towards a very important new phase of his life and a forever changed relationship with his parents. Last, but certainly not least, here comes the bride walking down the aisle accompanied by both of her parents because the same concept applies to both the bride and the groom concerning parent involvement in the marriage ceremony. You will see the bride walk around the groom seven times. Benedictions are said over the wine and both the man and the woman drink from the same cup (unsanitary but traditional). The man gives the woman the ring of nominal worth pronouncing in Hebrew the words: "*Behold you are consecrated to me with this ring according to the Law of Moses and Israel.*" I might add here that it is customary in Conservative and Reform wedding ceremonies for the bride and groom to exchange rings during the ceremony and for each one to repeat the same Hebrew words. The *Ketubah* or marriage contract is then read out loud. Usually it is read in both Hebrew and English. Seven blessings are then recited and family members and/or dear friends share in this part of the ceremony by being called up to the *Huppah* to recite a blessing.

AN ACT OF VIOLENCE?

The ceremony concludes with a wrapped glass being placed under the bridegroom's foot. He then crushes this glass with his foot. The symbolism behind this act makes us remember the destruction of the Temple, a major tragic event in Jewish history, even at a time of great joy. The Temple was the focus of Jewish worship in ancient times and was destroyed two times. Its final destruction came at the hands of the Romans in the year 70CE. Today, the only part still standing from that Temple is what is today commonly known as the Western or the Wailing Wall in Jerusalem. You often see photographs of throngs of people or a single person as the case may be, praying while standing in front of that holy spot.

As you view this finale act of the wedding ceremony, do not go into shock with the realization that you have just been witness to an act of minor violence. Keep in mind that the glass is flimsy and wrapped in a protective covering. No groom has ever gotten glass stuck in his shoe and foot and has had to be hospitalized before the reception. You will soon be able to see for yourself that the groom is walking without a limp. You will find yourself getting caught up in the loud exclamations of the phrase "*Mazel Tov*" which is Hebrew for

"Good Luck" as the newly weds make their way back down the aisle arm in arm with music playing in the background. Once the bridal party has walked out, you may leave your seat and go into the reception room. You have been seated throughout the entire ceremony. The guests never stand during any part of the wedding ceremony, not even when the bride makes her magnificent entrance.

YOU MAY DINE WITH HER BUT
YOU CANNOT DANCE WITH HER

As the wedding reception begins you are thinking serious eating and equally serious dancing (well not quite!). Before you can begin eating you must listen to a prayer which is uttered in Hebrew and which is said over the bread (*Challah*). This honor is usually given to a dad or granddad. The twisted bread looking like a braided sub sandwich large enough to feed all of Kosovo, if need be, is cut and the many course wedding meal can now begin. You are happy to see that there is no separate seating during the reception and are now waiting for the "dance music" to be played because you want to dance. Music is heard but it is unfamiliar and there appears to be no couples on the dance floor. It soon becomes apparent that there are definitely no couples dancing, but lots of people dancing in several groups. There are groups of men dancing in circle-like formations, and groups of women doing the same. Very often within the men's group you can spot several men doing Russian Cossack like jigs or holding someone on top of their shoulders. The women are also within their circles holding each other by the arms as they swing one another around. It seems that almost everyone is caught up in the great music and in the dances. At a certain point you will see the bride hoisted up on one chair and the groom hoisted up on another chair. As the groups of people carry the chairs closer to one another the bride and groom hold a handkerchief between them and sway to the music in their chairs.

A MIXTURE OF JOY AND GOD

At another point masks and toys appear on the dance floor. It almost seems like a combination of Halloween and Mardi Gras wrapped up into one big party. When asked what is the significance of bringing masks, Mickey Mouse ear sets, etc. to the dance floor of this wedding reception, the answer is a simple one. The whole object is to entertain the bride and groom and keep them smiling and happy on their special day. And the concept of separate is a great part of this special day. Men and women dancing together is closeness and sensual and sexual. Throughout the Orthodox Jewish wedding ritual the concept of having God be an integral part of this event is evident. There is always the need to be able to act and think clearly, with no distractions, and to always focus on the religious overtones of this event.

THE CONSERVATIVE WEDDING

When invited to a Conservative Jewish wedding and reception, almost everything you have just read will be in evidence. One major difference will be the elimination of the word separate. You will be able to sit with members of the opposite sex during the wedding ceremony and dance with whomever you wish. Traditional circle dances may or may not be incorporated into the festivities. On the whole the music and dancing will be conventional, familiar and what is in vogue at the time throughout the country. Another difference is the fact that in most cases the bride and groom do not fast on their wedding day, or at best will participate in a partial fast. You will be able to enjoy a cocktail and that stuffed mushroom with the groom during the cocktail hour. You will not be witness to the little ceremony between the bride and groom that took place before the actual wedding ceremony. You may also become aware of the fact that not every male will be wearing a skullcap during the entire event. Everyone will wear it during the ceremony, but not everyone, including the groom, will proceed to wear it for the remainder for the wedding party. The food served at this wedding will also be entirely kosher.

THE REFORM WEDDING

The real deviation becomes apparent when you are invited to attend a Reform Jewish wedding. In many instances, the marriage ceremony and reception will be held in a Conservative synagogue or a catering establishment where only kosher food will be served. There will be equally as many instances when the wedding will take place in a beautiful location not equipped to prepare and to serve kosher food, or quite simply kosher food can be served but your hosts have decided against that option. All restaurants and catering establishments will be able to order as many self-contained, individually wrapped kosher meals as are needed to satisfy the dietary needs of those guests who only eat kosher food. Just remember that when your invitation arrives with the food selection card included that has been especially created so that any guest who is in need of a kosher meal will be given the opportunity to order one, please do not select a kosher meal for yourself out of curiosity! These meals are extremely costly and most important of all, your hosts will think you have lost your mind!

Men who are followers of this branch of Judaism often do not wear skullcaps so only a handful will wear them during the wedding ceremony, let alone arrange for them to be provided to their guests. The wedding will usually be divided into the cocktail hour first, the ceremony and then the reception. Many members of both Conservative and Reform Judaism do also choose to have the ceremony first so that the bride can also enjoy the bulk of the wedding festivities with her family and friends.

DON'T TELL GRANDMA SHE IS NOT JEWISH!

You might also find yourself attending a mixed marriage wedding. Mixed marriages only take place among Conservative and Reform Jews. In this instance you may very well fall into the category of "family member" and not just "friend". The ceremony may very well be conducted by both a Rabbi and a member of the clergy from the other faith being represented in this union. I have had only had one opportunity to attend an inter-faith marriage and it was presided over by a Judge. The ceremony incorporated aspects of both religious backgrounds: the groom being walked down the aisle by both of his parents; the bride being walked down the aisle by her father as all of the guests stood up to honor her; a prayer in Hebrew; a beautiful speech by His Honor who was also a family friend; and the breaking of the glass. Most importantly, it captured the warmth, joy, love, intelligence and sincerity with which that particular couple had arrived at that special moment in time. The ceremony ended on a note oddly familiar to all wedding ceremonies – not a dry eye in the room and a loving and beaming couple walking down the aisle together.

I'VE GOT TO GET THE GET!

Unfortunately, no matter what branch of Judaism the bride and groom are from, many will not live happily ever after. These unions, which began amidst such pomp and circumstance and with such feelings of great hope and love, will have to be dissolved. At that time, not only will the couple have to deal with the emotionally and financially draining exercise of obtaining a civil divorce through our secular court system; they will also have to deal with the criteria established by Jewish law. Jewish law specifically asserts that only two ways exist to end a marriage. One way occurs upon the death of a spouse. The second way occurs when the soon to be ex-husband gives his soon to be ex-wife a religious document known as a get.

The giving of the get is one firm, immutable rule that has been handed down through the ages. Both the husband and the wife play a very specific role in this process. There is no room for creativity. Quite simply, it is the role of the husband to give the get and it is the role of the wife to receive a get. The get is dated, contains the names and addresses of the parties, and very importantly, allows for the wife to remarry. Of course, the husband is also free to remarry. As both participants look on, a scribe who has been carefully selected to write the entire document in the Hebrew language is painstakingly preparing the document. It should be added that two witnesses must also be present during this type of ceremony. Being the scribe in this proceeding is a real pressure job. If at any point the scribe makes a mistake then the entire task must begin again. There can be no cross outs and the use of whiteout is a taboo. The most important thing to be remembered from this process is that the husband is the only person on the face of this earth who can initiate the *giving of the get* to his wife and that this cannot be done unless the wife is in full agreement to receive the *get*. While our modern day court system is set up in such a way that it allows for either one or both parties to be absent on the day when the judgment of divorce that ends the union is actually signed; Jewish law requires that both parties be present. Not only must they both be present, but they also must indeed stand squarely in front of one another and look at each other while the get is being prepared.

Once the scribe has carefully finished preparing this document an odd event occurs. The piece of paper that was so carefully prepared by the scribe is now torn apart and the pieces gathered together and wrapped in a handkerchief. This is done so that no one subsequently will cast any aspersions on the validity of the *get*. The husband then delivers this parcel to his wife. If at the time the wife is living in an area so distant from the groom's habitat that it becomes physically impossible for her to be present in the room while the get is being prepared then the husband will have to use a messenger to deliver the get to his wife. In my husband's case, his get was taken from his hand and given to a man in the room who was on his way to Israel where he would then be able to deliver the get to my husband's soon to be ex-wife. It should be noted that the messenger must be present throughout the entire proceeding. Upon the termination of a marriage, the man and the woman are free to remarry as he or she chooses.

In our modern day society, the aim of this whole ancient process known as the *giving of the get* is to enable the newly divorced spouse to be free to remarry. It is extremely difficult to find a rabbi to marry a person who has been divorced and who cannot produce a get. In some instances, a Reform Rabbi will be willing to perform such a ceremony. In all cases a Conservative or Orthodox Rabbi will not agree to remarry an individual who cannot produce proof of a get. With this knowledge in hand, individuals engaged in divorce litigation will seek out the American judicial system as the vehicle of last resort to seek to compel a spouse to either *give or to accept a get.* Sitting in today's matrimonial courtrooms, it has become increasingly more common to hear a judgment of divorce pronounced along with the instructions from the court to both parties to obtain a get as soon as possible. It should always be remembered that the problems of the high divorce rate within the Jewish community, as well as that of the reluctant spouse who refuses to give or receive a get, are solvable.

CHAPTER THREE: Here Comes the Food
(Or Exactly What Is This Kosher Thing?)

If one were engaged in that famous word association test and were given the word Jewish, it is a safe bet that one of the first words that would quickly come to mind is the word Kosher. You cannot think Jewish for very long and separate it from the concept of Kosher. The word Kosher is so frequently used and seen, even being the component for a famous line in one of Shakespeare's plays, that it has become a familiar and comfortable vocabulary word for all of us. Now comes the major question. We have heard it, we have seen it, and we can even spell it correctly but yet there remains this major question whose answer must be explored. Exactly what is this kosher thing? Or, to put it another way, what does it mean when one of your Jewish friends tells you that he or she is adhering to the dietary laws of their religion.

I WANT TO MAKE THIS ANIMAL KOSHER – NOW WHAT?

As I have referred to in previous chapters, kosher is tied directly into the body of laws governing food. In particular, kosher applies to those foods that can be eaten and are not specifically forbidden to be ingested in the Bible. Not only can meat be gotten from specific animals (sheep and cows), but to make it more confusing, the meat can only be taken from specific sections of those "safe to eat" animals. Firstly, the animal must have been slaughtered by a *shochet,* a ritual slaughterer in a particular manner. Then this meat which is taken from a particular section of a particular animal must be rinsed, soaked and covered in salt to remove as much blood as is possible from the meat. This explains why the same turkey or chicken can start off as a non-kosher animal and end up as a kosher one after the slaughter; salting and removal of blood processes have been completed. As we say – it is all in the slaughter! Meat that is taken from the pig can never be eaten. Therefore, foods such as bacon, ham or sausage are considered "forbidden foods".

21

IS THIS A KOSHER RESTAURANT?

This meat thing is the real tricky part of the entire kosher issue and must be understood and taken into consideration quite seriously whenever you are planning to embark on a social activity (and what social activity does not involve food?) with your Jewish friends who do keep kosher. *"Keeping kosher"* is the lingo used to explain a person who is of the Jewish faith and is adhering always to the dietary laws of the religion. You cannot simply arbitrarily select your favorite neighborhood steak house or a restaurant belonging to one of a number of the famous steak house franchises established throughout our country. You are under a greater obligation to your friend. Unless the restaurant represents itself as being a kosher restaurant that is under strict Orthodox rabbinical supervision, your friend who keeps kosher will barely be able to have a glass of water in the restaurant. Such restaurants easily identify themselves by putting in writing with bold lettering in the store window what appears to be akin to an oath or a pledge. to anyone who is concerned about the need to eat in a strictly kosher restaurant. By writing the words *"this restaurant is under strict orthodox rabbinical supervision"* the restaurant owner has in a sense taken an oath to use, prepare and serve only kosher food. Bet you never noticed this, but you will now!

Depending on where you live and where you are visiting for a particular day or evening, you may be able to choose from a wide selection of kosher restaurants. Gone are the days when a kosher restaurant was a synonym for your neighborhood delicatessen that looked like a dingy diner at best. Of course, such "neighborhood" "delicatessens do still exist, but are certainly more modern and appealing than those that I ate in as a child, and do bring in the lunch crowd of all races and religions. There are now in existence many kosher Chinese, kosher Italian, kosher Japanese, as well as kosher steak and fish restaurants. In the exclusive "east end" section of New York City you can find many pricey, upscale kosher restaurants. Proud members of this group include Il Patrizio located at 206 East 63rd Street; Prime Grill located at 60 East 49th Street; Shallots located at 350 Madison Avenue, between 55th and 56th Streets, in the atrium of the Sony Building; and Levana which is located at 141 West 69th Street. Levana's is a special favorite of mine because it is where we hosted the celebration of my son's graduation from high school. Keep restaurants like this in mind if you are taking a group out to dinner from work to celebrate a special achievement, or are looking for an upscale place in which to dine. On the other end of the spectrum, in your predominantly Orthodox Jewish neighborhoods you can come across the kosher answer to McDonalds, which is actually a chain of restaurants known as McDavids. With the exception of the inexpensive McDavids food chain, all kosher restaurants tend to be between moderate and expensive in price range. When eating in any such establishment always remember that the taste of your favorite dishes may be a bit off due to the fact that ingredients may have been played with and /or altered in order to satisfy the dietary laws.

THE KOSHER FISH AND POULTRY GROUP

Fish can be eaten if they have both scales and fins and therefore it is forbidden to eat any type of shellfish such as lobster, shrimp, scallops, clams, mussels or other non-fin-and-scales fish (i.e. swordfish and sturgeon). Examples of fish that are considered kosher or safe to eat are tuna, whitefish, flounder, sole, trout, salmon, scrod, and sardine. Chicken, duck and turkey are your kosher-safe members of the poultry family. Above all else, please remember that milk products cannot be eaten with meat and poultry products. They can be eaten with your fish products. Consequently, all kosher meat and poultry foods can never be prepared with dairy products of any type.

THANK HEAVEN FOR THE PARVE FOODS

To substitute for dairy products, our kosher kitchens have introduced us to the wonderful world of *parve*. A kosher food falls into the *parve* column if it contains neither meat nor milk products. *Parve foods* are guest stars at all functions since those tantalizing chocolate, gooey desserts that arrive at your tables or are wheeled in as part of those awe inspiring Viennese tables are brought into creation through the magic of *parve* milk, cream, butter, etc. Your friends who keep kosher homes will have their refrigerators and pantries filled with *parve* items. After all, what would Thanksgiving be like if one could not duplicate that wonderful flavor of roasted turkey dripping with butter (Did I say butter? OOPS, my mistake-of course I mean dripping with *parve margarine*).

If you should ever find yourself invited to the home of a friend who keeps a strictly kosher home you will know in advance that all members of the meat, fish and poultry family ever brought into that particular home, prepared in that particular kitchen and eaten by family members and guests alike are all strictly kosher. The term "strictly kosher" means that all of the above have been certified to be kosher for they have been prepared for sale and consumption while being under orthodox rabbinical Jewish supervision. A rabbi (you will always find the name of the rabbi printed on the product) has certified that everything has been prepared in adherence with the law as set down in the Bible and that nothing forbidden has been used or has been in contact with a particular food product.

ONCE AGAIN -JUST WHAT FOODS ARE KOSHER?

The same holds true for non-meat, non-fish and non-poultry products. Even though they do not come from any of the "forbidden" food list, a strictly kosher person will only buy and consume those products that are made and sold in a "strictly kosher" store. These foods can also be found in your favorite supermarket but must have a marking that easily identifies the product as "strictly kosher". The most common marking is the letter u in a circle, which means that this product was prepared under orthodox supervision. This is a considered the Harvard of markings for identifying strictly kosher products. You will also come across this sign], as well as the letter "K" which stands for kosher. I must warn you again that strictly orthodox Jews will only eat foods with the letter u in the circle marking. which is known as the o-u marking. In addition, you will actually see the word "parve" written on a product. The products I am referring to are those familiar foods such as butter, margarine, milk, bread, cakes, cookies, sodas, juices, canned fruits and vegetables, cereals, pastas, frozen foods, nuts, ice cream and candy. Cheeses of all types (soft and hard) must have a kosher label to be considered a strictly kosher food. Be particularly careful to note that most hard cheeses are not kosher but that a company known as Miller has a large selection of assorted kosher cheeses hanging in the dairy section of most supermarkets. If your friend keeps only a "kosher-style" home they will not be checking for "kosher" markings on the foods that I have just listed. As you can see, one does not have to choose a specifically designated "kosher" store to shop kosher. If you were to stop reading now and look at the items that are currently sitting on your refrigerator shelves, as well as those items stocked in your pantry, you will be surprised to find out how many items have "kosher certification" on them. Amazing, is it not? You have been keeping a partially kosher home all of these years!

YOUR KOSHER COLLEAGUE

Here comes the area that presents the greatest opportunities for misinterpretation and which cries out for great sensitivity. Realizing the great selectivity and care that goes into keeping a kosher home and eating kosher while outside the home, you can now fully appreciate why your friend who is adhering to the dietary laws of the religion is quite standoffish about participating in the morning "breakfast club", the office birthday parties, the impromptu after work drinks and light snacks, as well as joining the group for Chinese food at lunch time. You can always include your friend with very little extra work. You can bring into the office bags of "kosher" marked bagels, "kosher" cheeses and "kosher" breads. Familiar brands such as Stella D'oro, Drakes, and Friehofers all have a kosher line of cookies and cakes. All Entenmanns products are kosher. Add any of these brands of donuts, cookies or cake selections when the group is setting up for their weekly breakfast group. Use only paper plates and plastic silverware for the cutting and serving of these kosher products.

You will see how easily and how happily your friends quickly become part of the office and out of the office eating events.

This is a birthday party-planning alert! If you want to surprise your friend with a birthday cake, seek out a kosher bakery from which to make the purchase. Please remember that all Carvel and Haagen Daas ice cream products are kosher (check the Haagen Daas Rum Raisin flavor because the last time I looked it did not have an O – U marking due to the rum extract used for the flavoring). Everyone can enjoy a freshly prepared Carvel ice cream cake. You will save both yourself and your friend from the embarrassment that unfolds when the birthday person quickly realizes that he or she will be unable to enjoy their own birthday cake!

There is one more thing to remember! Whenever you are being invited to your friend's home and volunteer to bring some food-related product, check to be certain that it is kosher. As was already discussed, this must also apply to your selection of drinks. If you are determined to bring something to eat and can find a kosher bakery you will discover that their selection of baked goods is on a par with those of your favorite bake shop. But shopping in a kosher bakery does come with a warning. Their baked goods are expensive. If you are comfortable with this route, remember that a gift of assorted cookies or a cake is always a welcome gift.

Many of your Jewish friends will tell you that they do keep a strictly kosher home and will eat only kosher food when outside of their home, but these same people will agree to join you in a restaurant that is not a kosher restaurant. These people will order only kosher foods with the full knowledge that they will not be served on kosher dishes, eaten with kosher silverware, or prepared with strictly kosher ingredients. They are trying to be accommodating and not be left out of what they perceive to be fun events. Keep this in mind and remember how extremely appreciative they would be if once in a while the decision was made to go to a strictly kosher restaurant. Do the right thing and alter the dining plans to accommodate everyone! One of my closest friends, who I like to view as the sister that I never had, was in a convent for nine years and left before taking her final vows. Our friendship has spanned the life and death of my son and all of the unbelievable joys and heartaches of life in between. She has been to many kosher restaurants on different occasions with us and each time has thoroughly enjoyed the dining experience along with the rest of us.

HIS HOME IS JUST LIKE MINE!

Finally, you may find that your friend does not even keep a kosher home, and indeed has come from a family that has traditionally not kept a kosher home. It may very well be that at this point in time you are far better versed in the laws of keeping kosher then is your friend. There will certainly be no problems eating anywhere or anything. You can easily invite your friend to your home and not have to worry about what to serve or what to serve it on. A few years ago my husband and I moved into a new community and after a while, as is often the case, our neighbors became our friends. They are a delightful, highly educated young couple who happen not to be Jewish. When the first time came to invite us to their home for a cocktail hour, our friend admitted that she had spent quite a bit of time on the phone with her mother who lives in the Midwest. Using an encyclopedia and a cookbook these two highly sophisticated and educated women spent hours trying to learn and understand just what this kosher thing is all about in order to know what foods could and could not be served. For the simple truth was that they had never before been faced with the situation of entertaining "kosher". Everything worked out fine. We were comfortable with the food situation, but someone who is strictly orthodox would never be able to feel comfortable eating in the home of anyone who did not keep a strictly kosher home, Jewish or not! You would literally have to make your entire kitchen kosher for such a person to eat in your home. Your oven would have to be prepared as a "kosher" oven, and all of your dishes, silverware, glassware and cooking utensils would also have to be set up as two of everything in terms of serving both kosher diary and kosher meat meals. Keep in mind that not all materials can be koshered. Earthenware materials can never be koshered. As you can see, if you do not keep a kosher home, it is entering the realm of the impossible to feel you can with comfort and in true honestly invite a person who is strictly kosher to eat in your home.

CHAPTER FOUR: Here Comes The Children

THE BRIS

It seems like only yesterday when you were heartily eating your first kosher meal and were getting caught up in the learning of those intriguingly new circle dances at your friend's wedding. Could it be possible that their first child was just born today? If you were told that it is a boy, you were also told in the next breath that a *Bris* would be held on the eighth day of his or her son's life. *Bris* is the Hebrew abbreviation for *Brit Milah* that translates into Covenant of Circumcision. The ceremony refers to the covenant between God and his people, and traditionally goes back to the days of the patriarch Abraham. At this time the newborn male is welcomed in to the Jewish faith. For no male is considered to be a Jew unless he is both born of a Jewish mother and circumcised according to the laws of Moses and Israel. Quite simply the ceremony consists of the removal of the foreskin of the penis. When questioning why this procedure must be performed on the eighth day of the little guy's life, it is because the number seven represents cycles of nature; there are seven days in a week. Eight, therefore, reflects that which is above, or beyond nature. The *eighth day of life* is firmly set in stone. There is once again no flexibility in carrying out this ancient ceremony. The only time when this procedure will be postponed is if it is deemed by his doctor that the infant was born with a condition that must first be treated before he can be well enough to withstand the circumcision ceremony.

Illness aside, the performance of the circumcision takes place as scheduled. If that eighth day of life happens to fall on a Sabbath or a major Jewish holiday, so be it. My own son was born on a Saturday evening. After it was determined by our family rabbi that his birth occurred after sundown we were told that the *Bris* had to be held on the following Sunday. The *Bris* is a joyous celebration, second only in preparation and effort to his *Bar Mitzvah*. You can be certain that once the excited new father makes the grandparent calls, the next call to be placed is to a qualified *Mohel* who will be the one to carry out the procedure. A *Mohel* is a person who has had to successfully complete medical training in this procedure at an accredited hospital, either in this country or very often in Israel. He is most probably also a rabbi.

The *Bris* will more likely than not be held in the home of the parents or grandparents, as the case may be. Because the focus is on the eighth day of life, the odds are great that it will occur on a weekday. If the *Bris* must take place on a Saturday, which is the Jewish Sabbath, please do not be offended if you are not invited. Remember that orthodox Jews do not drive on the Sabbath, nor do they wish for anyone else to drive in order to accommodate them. If you are an extremely close friend, then you may very well be told that sleeping arrangements are being made so that you will be able to arrive before sundown on Friday and be able to be a part of the *Bris* ceremony on Saturday.

If the *Bris* is being held on a weekday the time of the *Bris* depends upon the schedule of the *Mohel* and whether or not it is the preference of the family to serve breakfast, brunch or lunch to their guests. In any case, the invitation is always a verbal one due to the short time frame involved. The beauty and joy and uniqueness of this first event in the life of the little fella is an opportunity not to be missed. Indeed, when you arrive for the *Bris* you will probably be surprised to see how many family members and friends are in attendance. It is at this time that baby gifts are brought to the newborn, or arrangements have been made to send a gift. If the *Bris* is being held on the Sabbath please remember that no money can be exchanged on that day, nor do Orthodox Jews carry anything such as a wrapped baby gift. Either arrange to send your gift or present it before the Sabbath begins or after it ends. Remembering that money is always an appropriate gift, here is a great opportunity to give your gift in multiples of eighteen. Eighteen is the Hebrew word for "life" and this is a gift acknowledging and celebrating a new life!

A WORD OF CAUTION!

This may not be the time to opt for front row orchestra seats. If someone has never witnessed this actual minor medical procedure-the onset of queasiness is not unusual. Many years ago I was working with a young man who came into the office one day with the announcement that his wife had given birth to twin boys and that the entire office was being invited to attend the *Bris* the following week. When we arrived at his home on the day of the *Bris* there was a large overflowing crowd. We were all ushered into the living room where the two ceremonies would take place. An extremely tall co-worker, who was not Jewish and totally unprepared for what the *Bris* ceremony entailed, had positioned himself against the living room wall. As the first circumcision began, we all heard him (not the baby) let out a small painful sickly cry of "Oh, No!" and immediately leave the room. Due to the fact that there is removal of some bodily part from the baby, you will witness the natural aftermath of any such procedure. The baby will cry even as the *Mohel*, while putting a wine-soaked piece of gauze into the baby's mouth, is assuring the assembled group that this procedure is not hurting the baby. No *Mohel* has ever been able to convince me of that fact but I will let you be your own judge. Very often, depending upon whom the *Mohel* is, an informative and humorous dialogue by the *Mohel* will precede the ceremony.

WHO IS THAT PALE PERSON HOLDING THE BABY?

In my opinion, the cutest part of the ceremony is when the "guest of honor" appears with a miniature skullcap tied to his head. He has been sequestered away until the time of the ceremony. When the ceremony is about to begin, most modern day *Mohels* will secure the baby to a small board and place baby and board on a table. The *Sandak* is the honored person (in most instances a grandfather) who will steady the board and baby as the procedure begins. When my own son was circumcised, it was almost always the duty of the *Sandak* to hold the baby in his arms while the ceremony took place. I can still remember the loving but equally pale look on my father's face as he held my son. My father had dropped out of a pre-medical course in college because he could not stand the sight of blood, but is there anything more powerful than the bond of love between a grandfather and his grandchild?

THE NAMING CEREMONY

A second and concluding part of the ceremony occurs when the child is given his Hebrew names, and a benediction over the wine is said. After the ceremony is completed a major effort will be made to put the baby to sleep. So if you want to get a good look at him, it may be advisable to see him before the ceremony when he will be in a really good mood. At that time you can offer him words of encouragement and advice. After the ceremony and after you have partaken in the festive celebration meal, you will notice that all of the invited quests will begin to say their good-byes. This occurs because in many instances everyone is rushing back to their job and the immediate family members as well as the newest member of the Jewish faith are exhausted.

Each member of the Jewish religion, both girl and boy alike, are named in Hebrew. They will more often than not be named after a departed loved one. The great majority of your Jewish friends will be Askenazim Jews who are Jews whose ancestors settled in Northern France, Germany, Poland and Eastern Europe. The descendants of these Jews make up the bulk of the Jewish population in America and will only name their children after departed loved ones. No child will ever be named after a living parent or grandparent. The opposite is true of those people who are known as Sephardic Jews. The Sephardic Jews believe it is a great honor to name their child after a living grandparent. The words Junior and Senior will never follow the name.

While I was growing up not only did I think that the whole world was Jewish, I also thought that there were only Askenazim Jews in the world! It was only when I grew up, was introduced to my future husband, had my parents ask me if his last name was indeed a Jewish name because no one in their synagogue or neighborhood ever had a name like that –that I slowly began to learn about the customs of the Sephardim. The Sephardic Jews had their origins in Spain and in

North Africa. My husband was born and raised in Morocco, which was a French protectorate for many years. His first language was Arabic and he was schooled in French. Yiddish is unknown to the Sepharim. He never tires of teasing me that our marriage falls into the category of mixed marriages!

On the first Sabbath following the birth of a daughter, her father along with his family and friends will go to the synagogue where at a particular time in the service, a ceremony will take place to name this new baby. The baby girl does not have to be present during this ceremony. The appearance of the newborn for her naming depends to a large part upon what branch of Judaism that family has embraced. It is extremely rare to see the baby brought to an orthodox synagogue but it is a more common practice among conservative and reform Jews. After the traditional Saturday morning services are completed, it is most common to have the entire congregation invited to join the family and their friends in what is known as "A Kiddush". It begins with the prayer over the wine (thus the name Kiddush), a prayer over the chollah bread and then flows over into a festive luncheon or brunch as the case may be. You will find yourself partaking in an assortment of cakes, breads, fishes, wine, and salads to celebrate the naming which has just taken place.

It is important to understand that the Hebrew names that each baby boy and girl are given are not just "pet" names, nor are they names only to be used in a "synagogue" setting. Often over the years I have had more than one of my non-Jewish friends tell me that he or she knows the pet name and/or the synagogue name of a mutual Jewish friend. These Hebrew names are the actual names of a beloved deceased relative that the parents have chosen to give to their newborn child. In fact, the process is performed in reverse. First, the parents decide who their new daughter or son will be named for, know what the Hebrew names will be, and then in most instances a great effort is made to match the English name to the Hebrew name in terms of what letter of the alphabet the Hebrew name begins with. For example, my son's Hebrew name was Abraham Meier and so the decision was made to give him the English names Alan Mark.

33

Members of the orthodox branch of Judaism may very well give their children only Hebrew names. My son went all through private Hebrew education and the simple truth is that I did not even know the English names of some of his friends because they always called one another by their Hebrew names. When my son was little he once asked me if all of the children born in Israel were also given English names along with their Hebrew names. It seemed quite obvious to him that if Jewish-American children had both English and Hebrew names, then the flip side should also apply by giving English names to children born in a country where Hebrew is the official language. The answer was of course no, but I can see how he or someone else might ponder the same question.

Now that you are fully versed in the why and how and wherefore of a BRIS – you might be asking yourself how this can occur if you are invited to an inter-faith BRIS and you know that the mother is not Jewish. Unless the mother has undergone a conversion, Jewish law dictates that the child cannot be considered to be Jewish. Due to the fact that in today's society almost all of the newborn males are circumcised anyway while still in the hospital, many inter-faith couples make the decision to have the circumcision done on the eighth day in accordance with Jewish law, whether or not the mother has undergone a proper conversion! This way they are incorporating a part of the father's heritage into the new family unit. This will be done, of course, more for show than for substance.

THE BAR AND BAT/BAS MITZVAH

As you stood by as a loving and interested witness, major rites of passage were just experienced by these tiniest and newest members of the Jewish religion. The next time that these little boys and girls will find themselves in such a fishbowl existence Jewish religion-wise is when they are *Bar Mitzvahed* and *Bat* or *Bas-Mitzvah*. These are major events in their lives and depending on the type of families they have been raised in and the type of communities they live in, you will find that the planning and celebration of these events often exceed that of a wedding. You will indeed be receiving a formal invitation to these celebrations that are divided into two parts: the synagogue services and the reception to be held afterwards.

Through the years I have often heard many people say that for a myriad of reasons they could not attend the two parts of the event so they opted for the reception with its food and dancing and socializing that is equal to that of a wedding reception. The *Bar Mitzvah* or *Bat* or *Bas Mitzvah* reception will either immediately follow the services, or be held on a Saturday evening or a Sunday afternoon or evening. If you do not attend the actual services you would truly have missed the best part. Knowing this, try to make every effort to attend. When attending the actual service appropriate dress would be business suits for the men and business suits or dresses for the women. You will find that no young man or woman shines brighter than on this day. You will find them as a group poised, eager, studious, spiritually inspired, beaming with pride on their accomplishment, joyously happy and somehow almost grown-up! But the best part of all is that for that one day and/or weekend as the case may be the precarious "teen-ager" actually gets along with and loves everyone.

HE IS A MAN TODAY

Whereas the carrying out of the ceremony known as the *Bris* welcomed the newborn male into the Jewish religion, it is the carrying out of the ceremony commonly known as the *Bar Mitzvah* that will welcome him into adulthood in the eyes of the Jewish community. Among the orthodox and conservative branches of Judaism, a major acknowledgment to the young *Bar Mitzvah* that he is viewed as an adult by the Jewish community is that now he can be counted as part of the quorum of ten men that must be present before the service can start. On occasion, I have been in an orthodox synagogue filled with at least twenty women and less then ten men and have heard the comment being made that there are not enough people present to begin the service. And I might add that these occasions took place at times in my life when I was no where near goal weight in Weight Watcher terminology!

Traditionally, it has been taught that a boy had reached adulthood at the age of thirteen. To celebrate this occasion, the boy is called up to read from the *Torah* portion and/or the *Haftorah* portion that take place during the traditional Saturday morning synagogue services. As was mentioned earlier, the concept of the word Torah consists of many layers. It can mean all of the laws on a particular subject, or it can mean the total of Jewish law. The ceremony will most often take place on a Saturday morning. We held my son's *Bar Mitzvah* on the Thursday of Thanksgiving. We did this for the particular reason that a large part of my family is orthodox, as were my son's friends and my son for that matter. Given this situation, none of these people would have been able to get in a car and ride to the service and join us in the celebration of this joyous event that took place immediately after the service, if it had taken place on the Sabbath. In our case the downside was that some of our guests could not attend because of previous, etched in stone Thanksgiving commitments. We certainly understood, but they were still greatly missed. A *Bar Mitzvah* can be held on any day when the Torah is read and the Torah is also read on Thursday mornings.

THE CEREMONY

The Saturday morning *Torah* readings are the highlight of the service. Woven through the selected *Torah* portion for the day are the heart and soul of your Biblical history and moral and religious advice. As the Jewish year unfolds, a different Torah and *Haftorah* portion is read on each Sabbath. The *Haftorah* reading is chosen because it has some connection with the *Torah* reading. The public reading of the *Torah* is divided into 54 Sabbaths. Normally, before and after the reading, the scroll is taken in procession around the synagogue where you will see both men and women alike try to touch and kiss the *Torah* with their lips or their prayer books. The proud *Bar Mitzvah* boy will almost always be in the middle of this procession. At some point, usually after it is brought back to the podium area, the *Torah* is raised up in the air to show the congregation. You will find that you do not have to work hard to locate the *Bar Mitzvah* boy. He will be seated up on the podium or dais along with the Rabbi and Cantor who are officiating over the service. In many cases, one of them has been the boy's teacher for his special *bar mitzvah* training. This is a good thing because he can be there for assistance and encouragement of his student as the service proceeds.

On those Sabbaths when the synagogue is not hosting a *Bar Mitzvah*, the ceremony comprising the reading of the *Torah* portion will be done as a group effort from amongst the synagogue worshippers. Each reader recites a prayer before and after his reading and normally at least seven men are called up to read. The language that the *Torah* is read in is a very difficult one for the *Torah* has been written and therefore must be read in the Aramaic language. The *Bar Mitzvah* boy will read as much or as little of the *torah* and H*aftorah* as his ability and training will allow. While watching this service unfold, you will quickly become aware of the fact that close male family members such as a father, older brother, uncle and grandfather are being given the honor of being called up to the podium to read the prayers. A gentleman (think of him as the master of ceremonies) will call each person to the podium by calling out his Hebrew name. This procedure will be carried out in orthodox and conservative *Bar Mitzvah* ceremonies.

This is truly an awesome task being asked of the young man since it is important to never loose sight of the fact that the *Torah* is not written in Hebrew which is the language that has been studied by the *Bar Mitzvah* boy during his many years of attending Hebrew School, but in Aramaic (a language spoken in the ancient world). Now you can understand why even though the studying of Hebrew has been an intricate part of the education of Jewish boys and girls, there arises a great need for individual *Bar Mitzvah* or *Bat Mitzvah* lessons for at least a year prior to the big day. In most cases, children will begin Hebrew school as early as five years of age. This attendance takes place in an after school setting and on Sundays as well. Many families that make up both the orthodox and conservative branches of Judaism will chose to send their children to all day Hebrew Day Schools where half of the school day is devoted to the study of all of the secular subjects and the other half is devoted to Hebrew studies.

Somewhere near the end of the service, the Rabbi will give his weekly sermon, but it will of course be directed to the *Bar Mitzvah* boy and will incorporate the lessons learned from the *Torah* reading of the morning. The *Bar Mitzvah* boy will also speak (in English). It is customary for the young man to thank his family for everything that they have done to help bring him to this day. Often the young man will go on to speak about the lessons learned from the Torah portion he just read. He appears before you beautifully dressed in a new suit, shirt and tie and a beautiful kipah and *tallis*. A *tallis* is worn by adult males and is an oblong piece of cloth with knotted fringes on each corner. It may be made of wool or silk. Amongst the orthodox, the *Bar Mitzvah* boy will only wear the *tallis* on that day. He is not supposed to wear it again until after he is a married man. He will, however, always be given one whenever called up to the podium to recite any prayer before and after *torah* readings.

WHAT SHOULD I WEAR?
WHAT SHOULD I GIVE? (THINK "13")

It is important to remember that gifts are not to be brought to the synagogue. The gift giving takes place at the reception where you should come dressed as if you were attending a wedding reception. The one exception to this will be the reception hosted immediately after the services where business dress is in order. Whatever type of reception you are attending, you can either bring money to the reception, or send your gift; with the exception of those orthodox *Bar Mitzvah* receptions being held on Saturday afternoons. In those cases, the laws of the *Sabbath* must be strictly adhered to. You will not find a gift table at any of these receptions. If you have opted for money, you can most definitely give your gift in multiples of eighteen. When selecting a gift to send, think in terms of a thirteen-year-old! A gift certificate from a department store or a bookstore is an appropriate gift as is a gift of religious significance if you know the family and know that this particular young person will go on to incorporate their religious training into their daily lives. There are many stores that sell only articles of Jewish religious significance. A hand made kipah with either his English or Hebrew name stitched onto it, a beautiful selection of books in Hebrew, or a *Kiddush cup* are just a few suggestions. My son's favorite *Bar Mitzvah* gift came from a young couple who had bought four tickets to an upcoming New Jersey Devils ice hockey game. They asked my son to select a friend and after having Sunday brunch at my home, off all four of them went to the Devils game.

THE ORTHODOX GIRL

Although girls are considered to be religiously mature at the age of twelve, there is no ceremony of equivalent style and significance held in your orthodox communities. In many instances, the family will hold a special party in honor of their daughter turning either twelve or thirteen, but there will be no accompanying religious ceremony. Remember that among the orthodox a woman can still not be counted in a quorum. Women are never called up to the podium. They will never be asked to participate in any part of the reading of the *Torah* and/or H*aftorah*. There is segregated seating. Indeed, in many orthodox synagogues the men are seated downstairs while the women sit and pray in a specially built balcony section. When I was a young child, my favorite day of the week was Saturday when my three older boy cousins who I adored and who ranged in age anywhere from ten to eighteen years older than me, would swing by and take me with them to our little orthodox synagogue. I remember feeling so special sitting next to them as the only girl in a sea of all boys and men. I loved the feeling that I could do this because as little as I was I knew that very soon I would be relegated to the segregated "women's section."

THE CONSERVATIVE AND REFORM BAS
AND BAT MITZVAH

Among the conservative and reform branches of Judaism, girls are *Bas* or *Bat Mitzvah* at either ages twelve or thirteen. They undergo many years of Hebrew school training, as well as special private lessons to adequately prepare them for their *Bas* or *Bat Mitzvah*. They are called up to the podium, read from the *Torah* and/or *haftorah* and do give a speech to the congregation. In many instances, the religious ceremony will take place as a part of the Friday evening services where the *Torah* and/or *haftorah* are never read. At these events you will the *Bas* or *Bat Mitzvah* girl begin the service by lighting the Sabbath candles. It should be mentioned here that every Friday night before the Sabbath begins, it is the specific job of the Jewish mother to light the candles to symbolize peace and joy. This ritual is accompanied by the saying of a prayer over the candles while her head is covered.

The Friday night service will be a short one. If the *Bas* or *Bat Mitzvah* is being incorporated into the weekly Saturday morning services, it will be of much longer length. Whichever day the ceremony takes place, afterwards there will be a festive reception hosted by her proud parents that could again pass as a wedding reception. For appropriate dress as well as for gift giving, follow all of the rules and suggestions outlined for a *Bar Mitzvah*. In addition, you now have the flexibility of giving jewelry as a gift to this teenager. You will never have a problem being able to find out what is in vogue in jewelry for teenage girls. Such a gift will always be greatly appreciated and used.

THE REFORM CONFIRMATION

Finally, you may have heard, however rarely, the word "confirmation" used to describe a ceremony and celebration for young Jewish men and women. Among the reform branch of Judaism there are some reform congregations who will hold a service when all teenagers who have attended their religious after school centers reach the age of sixteen. Sixteen is the age of graduation for these young men and women. Very small pockets of reform Jews, as well as those who belong to what has come to be known as the progressive movement in Judaism, embrace. this very secular connotation and this type of ceremony. It s more like a graduation service then a Bar or Bas Mitzvah service and the receptions may not be quite as elaborate.

CHAPTER FIVE: Here Comes The Holidays

(Or Why Are They Wishing One Another
A Happy New Year in September?)

We Americans can almost recite our list of holidays backward in our sleep! These days are sacred and special and most important of all, our place of work is closed! It got even better when Congress gave birth to the best of all news: the three-day weekend! What creativity, what joy! We understand our holidays; we can depend on them taking place on or very close to the same date, and in the same month each year. But, alas, how alien and confusing everything suddenly becomes when we try to understand the world of the Jewish holidays.

JUST HOW MANY HOLIDAYS DO YOU HAVE?

A myriad of holidays make up the "Jewish calendar" which is calculated according to lunar months. The names of the months, for purposes of getting the correct spelling for those difficult Sunday New York Times cross word puzzles, are: Nissan, Iyyar, Sivan, Tammuz, Av, Elul, Tishri, Heshvan, Kislev, Tevet, Shevat and Adar. For whatever the rationale, whenever a leap year occurs, two months of Adar are celebrated. The calendar is calculated from the time of Adam in 3760 BCE. Because the year 5000 began on September 1, 1239, the current year can be calculated by deducting 1240 from the secular year and adding 5000. For example, I am writing this in the year 2001. If I were to subtract 1240 from 2000, and then add 5000, the answer to this equation is 5761. Thus, while the non-Jewish year is 2001, the Jewish year running fairly concurrently with it is 5761. For dates between September and December, an additional year is added. For a moment, imagine twins being born late on the night of August 31, 2000. While the one twin is born at 11:59 p.m. and has the year of birth recorded as the year 5761, the other twin is born at 12:01 a.m. and has the year of its birth recorded as 5762. I have always found that quite remarkable and the birth of the twins story as a great way to remember this "glitch" in the Jewish calendar. For our purposes, I will touch briefly on each holiday that takes place in the Jewish calendar in terms of how it is celebrated, the customary words and phrases associated with each holiday, and some great recipes to go along with the holiday festivities.

HAPPY NEW YEAR!

Let us begin with *Rosh Hashanah*, which is the celebration of the Jewish New Year. It is celebrated on Tishri 1, which traditionally falls somewhere between early September and early October. Because it is the Jewish New Year, simply wish your friend *A Very Happy and Healthy New Year!* It is a two-day holiday that the Orthodox and most Conservative Jews will celebrate by adhering to most of the rules of the Sabbath. Reform Jews will celebrate these holidays strictly, but most will ride to and from the synagogue and not all of the rules of the *Sabbath* will be followed. Some Reform Jews will only observe the first day of *Rosh Hashanah*. Please keep in mind that because the first and last two days of Jewish holidays are celebrated like a *Sabbath*, you will always see groups of people walking to and from their synagogues during the following holiday celebrations: on *Rosh Hashanah*, on *Yom Kippur*, on the first and last two days of *Sukkot*, on the first and last two days of *Passover*, as well as the first and last two days of *Shavuot*.

If you should find yourself entertaining during the period of the Jewish New Year, and would like to prepare a dish that is often made and associated with this holiday, then let me suggest a great recipe that is often prepared for holiday guests:

MOM'S BRISKET

1. Buy this very expensive cut of meat in a kosher butcher shop.
2. Place the meat in a large roasting pan and sear the meat on top of the oven for ten minutes per side.

3. Cube three onions and place on the bottom of a roasting pan. If you wish, you may also add cut up potatoes and carrots, so that the appearance is somewhat like an Irish stew. Rub in paprika over the meat.
4. Cover and cook in a 400-degree oven for two and half-hours.
5. After cooking for one half-hour, pour water over the meat.
6. Once done, let the meat cool on a platter.

Remembering that the celebration of any New Year is always associated with everyone's sincere wishes for a happy, healthy and "sweet" New Year, especially sweet desserts are the order of the day. Mom would always prepare a particular dessert that was heavily laden with dates (the fruit associated with the land of Israel) to give the dessert that extra sweet taste. This dessert has been enjoyed by our family for several generations and has been served at many family gatherings. It is lovingly referred to by many of Mom's nieces, nephews, grandnieces and grandnephews as:

AUNT JEANETTE'S SQUARES

1. The ingredients (**to be measured strictly and not stingily per MOM**) are one and a half pounds of walnuts, one eight-ounce package of pitted dates, three eggs, one cup of sugar, one cup of flour, one teaspoon baking powder, and one teaspoon of vanilla extract.
2. Cut up the walnuts and dates into small pieces and set aside.
3. Sift the flour and baking powder and set aside.
4. Beat the eggs and add one cup of sugar and one teaspoon of vanilla to the eggs.
5. Mix in the walnuts and dates with #4.
6. Gradually add the sifted flour and baking powder. At this point it appears to look like "one big mush."
7. Grease an 8" square baking pan and pour the entire mixture into the pan and bake for one-half hour at a 350 degree oven until the top appears to be golden brown.

8. Sprinkle confectionery sugar over the top and bake for an additional 45 minutes at 350 degrees.
9. When done, remove from the oven, let cool, and then cut into squares. This recipe yields approximately 40 pieces. To add a festive holiday touch to this dish, Aunt Jeanette's squares has always been presented in multi-colored paper cupcake holders.

JUDGEMENT AND REPENTANCE
(THE DAY OF ATONEMENT)

It is believed that all human beings are judged on *Rosh Hashanah* and if it so happens that you are dealt an evil decree, you are given ten days to repent through prayer. These ten days culminate with the observance of *Yom Kippur*, a day of complete fasting and general abstinence. It is considered to be the most holy day of the Jewish year. It takes place on Tishri 10 after the ten days of penitence. No work may be performed and no food or drink may be consumed from sundown when the holiday begins with the night known as *Kol Nidre* (the name of a very important prayer that is recited three times in the synagogue on that evening) until roughly twenty-five hours later when night falls. The appropriate thing to say is *Have A Good And An Easy Fast* as your friend rushes out of work early (usually no later than 3 p.m.) to be able to go home, eat a fairly substantial meal and prepare to be in attendance at the early evening synagogue services that will usually begin around 6 p.m.

I like to view *Yom Kippur* as akin to last licks in a baseball game. You are given one more opportunity to put your best efforts forward to change whatever evil decree you may have been dealt and to be entered into the *Book of Life* for another year. Your day is spent in prayer and asking for forgiveness for all of the sins that you may have or indeed did commit. You hope and pray that you will be given another opportunity to live a good and a decent life and to truly do the work of God while here on earth. At the end of the evening *Yom Kippur* service a festive buffet of foods may be served to the entire congregation and everyone may *break the fast* together and once again wish each other a very happy and a healthy New Year. It has evolved that many families host a *break the fast* dinner at their homes and invite friends and family, Jew and non-Jew alike to join in the celebration of a new year and of hopefully new beginnings.

After having not eaten for approximately twenty-six hours, it is customary to *break the fast* with breakfast foods such as orange juice, a fresh pot of coffee (no instant coffee this night!), hard and soft cheeses, chollah bread, cookies, cakes and fishes of your choice. Mom would always prepare a fantastic cold pickled fish dish. Now, as I think back to our little kitchen in the Bronx, with its small table, I can never remember happier meals than when we would sit down to *break the fast* together and Mom would set out as the guest of honor, her fantastic pickled fish in an old Pyrex deep round bowl. Nothing ever tasted as good as that fish, or was eaten as quickly and praised as much as that fish! Mom had some difficulty in remembering all of the ingredients and steps of preparation for this particular dish. Help arrived in the form of a close friend who still prepares this dish. So, thanks to Mom's good friend, Sunny, the following is the recipe for:

SUNNY'S PICKLED FISH
(JUST LIKE MOM USED TO MAKE IT)

The ingredients are one and a half cups of vinegar, one half cup of sugar, one teaspoon of salt, two medium sized onions that are finely diced, one tablespoon of pickling spices, three cups of water, one and a half pounds of yellow pike cut into two inch slices, and one and a half pounds of whitefish cut into two inch slices.

1. Place the fish in a four-quart pot and add salt, water, and one onion and bring to a boil.
2. After it boils, simmer for fifteen minutes. Then discard the fish head and carefully remove the fish and place it in a deep bowl.
3. Pour three and a half cups of the fish broth (created in #3) into a four-quart pot. Add the vinegar, sugar and spices and bring to a boil. Once it has boiled, cook for an additional five minutes.

4. Remove the fish and place it in a separate bowl. Then proceed to strain the liquid mixture over the fish.
5. Chill in the refrigerator for twenty-four hours. Keep in mind that this fish can remain fresh for up to two weeks.

THEY ALL DECIDED TO GO ON OVERNIGHTS THIS WEEK!

The next holiday, *Sukkot*, is one that you may be familiar with because it is easy to spot the observance of this holiday. The holiday commands the Jewish people to "dwell in booths" over an eight day period to commemorate the time when the Jewish people wandered in the wilderness before reaching the Promised Land. This is a time when, if you live in or near Jewish neighborhoods, you will begin to see little structures appearing that are akin to small huts with thatched roofs. They are erected outside Jewish homes and on the premises of all synagogues.

A GREAT FALL TRIP

If you live anywhere near Brooklyn, New York let me suggest an interesting fall day trip. Plan to visit the area known as the Williamsburg section of Brooklyn, New York, sometime during this weeklong celebration. An extremely large orthodox group of Jews, known as *Hasidim* (see definition in Chapter VII) live in this area. Since they reside in apartment buildings, in order to fulfill the obligations of this holiday, they will erect *Sukkohs* on their fire escapes. It makes for quite a visual to walk down their neighborhood streets on a beautiful fall day and observe the celebration of *Sukkot*.

Truly observant Jews will eat all of their meals in the *Sukkah*. Jews of Conservative and Reform persuasion will try to eat as many of their meals as is possible in the *Sukkah*. The *Sukkah* must be built to conform to exact specifications. It may not surprise you to learn that in this modern age we do have prefabricated *Sukkahs* that vary greatly in price depending upon the size and comfort level you have in mind. Being that the holiday occurs in the early fall many of the children consider this to be the ultimate overnight if they can successfully convince their parents to allow them to both eat and sleep in the *Sukkah* throughout the eight day observance of the holiday. If you are a member of a profession where you have a lot of contact with children, do not be surprised if you witness a major outbreak of colds amongst children celebrating this holiday.

Sukkot ends with the celebration of *Simhat Torah, which* is basically the celebration of the *Torah*. It was always a special day for us because my son was born on this holiday and we would always celebrate his birthday at this time, along with of course the celebration of his secular birthday. Yes, it is indeed true that many Jewish people will observe and celebrate their birthday on both the secular and Jewish calendar dates. As for the celebration of *Simhat Torah*, large parties are held in the synagogues where anywhere from mini sized to large sized *Torahs* are carried around as everyone sings and dances (circle dancing, of course). And for all of you who are wondering what to say to your friends, simply wish them a good holiday. It was always on *Simhat Torah* when Mom would prepare and serve her sensational stuffed cabbage. We simply could not get enough of it and would demand that she make it again and serve it as an appetizer during the cocktail hour that would always precede our traditional family Thanksgiving Day dinner. We were so fanatical about this that when the time came for my parents to retire to Florida and the need arose for them to have to fly to New Jersey from Florida in order to be able to spend Thanksgiving Day with us, the scenario would go as follows. Mom would have to prepare this dish in Florida. freeze it and then fly with their luggage, with the stuffed cabbage slowly defrosting, and with Dad to celebrate Thanksgiving Day in New Jersey.

MOM'S SENSATIONAL STUFFED CABBAGE

1. The ingredients are three pounds of chopped meat, two small heads of cabbage (together they should not to exceed five pounds), two eggs, one large lemon, two tablespoons of sugar,

one cup of white rice (uncooked), three medium sized onions, two Macintosh apples, one large can of tomato sauce and two small cans of tomato sauce, and a teaspoon of pepper. Please note that no salt is added to this recipe because we are using kosher meat and part of the koshering process involves adding salt to the meat, so please adjust accordingly if you are not going to be using kosher meat

2. Put the cabbage in the freezer and take it out to defrost the night before you will be using it. When ready to use you will see that the cabbage leaves will simply peel off as if you are peeling skin from a grape.

3. Place the meat in a pan and set that aside.

4. Beat the eggs and add the pepper to the eggs.

5. Add the rice to a glass of steaming hot water.

6. Grate in your onion, the one apple and add all of this to #3, #4 and #5. Mix well.

7. Use your largest cooking pot and cut up the two onions, grate in one apple and pour in a large can of tomato sauce.

8. Prepare each piece of stuffed cabbage by peeling off one cabbage leaf, and by stuffing it with a rolled small hamburger shaped portion of meat. Wrap the cabbage leaf around the meat and place the piece gently into the bottom of the pot. Repeat until everything is used up.

9. If you have any cabbage left over, simply cut it up and place it into the cooking pot.

10. Cook in a large covered pot for one and half-hours. When it starts to cook, it should be on a larger flame. At the beginning squeeze in the one lemon and add two tablespoons of sugar. In a short while reduce the flame to medium and let it cook.

11. If you see that the gravy is not thick enough, simply add another can of tomato sauce.

12. If you are one of those people who love to soak up gravy with your favorite fresh bread, this is you big chance. Enjoy!

Toby R. Serrouya

THIS IS NOT OUR CHRISTMAS

The eight-day celebration of the winter festival of lights, *Hanukkah*, or as it is sometimes spelled, *Chanukah*, is perhaps the best known of all of the Jewish holidays to non-Jews. It is commonly known as *The Festival of Lights*. It has achieved this celebrity status because it does happen to fall out in the wintertime (on Kislev 25) and is very close to the observance of Christmas. It can occur as early as late November, but will more often than not take place sometime during the month of December. How early or late the holiday will take place depends on how the Jewish lunar calendar is running in a given year.

This holiday goes back to post-biblical times and the Maccabee victory over the Hellenists which coincided with the miraculous burning of the holy oil, that was stored in the ancient Temple, for eight days rather than for the one day that it was expected to last. This extra burning time proved to be a Godsend for the Jewish warriors who were living at the Temple, as the battle was raging on. You will find that this holiday is celebrated in all Reform, Conservative and Orthodox households. It is now celebrated quite differently, though, than in the low-key manner of my own childhood.

When I was growing up, each family had their own *menorah* as we do today. A *menorah* is an eight-branch candleholder with an additional center candle known as the *shamas*. The *shamas* is used to light the other candles. One candle, and of course the *shamas*, is lit for each night of the holiday. The lighting ceremony consists of prayers being said as the candles are lit and with songs being sung after the lighting has taken place. On the last night, as all of the candles have been lit, including the *shamas*, it does make for a beautiful site. As a child I would receive a gift during this holiday, and would always give my parents each a gift. During at least one night of this holiday, my mother would be certain to prepare and serve potato *latkes* (potato pancakes) with gobs of freshly made applesauce, or with sour cream. This was my personal favorite part of the holiday and I want to share this wonderful recipe with you.

MOM'S POTATO LATKES

1. The ingredients are five potatoes (use Idaho Baking Potatoes), two eggs, a "dash" of salt and pepper (whatever that means!), and one-third cup of matzo meal. This recipe will yield six to eight servings.
2. Grate the five potatoes and mix in the two eggs with the salt and the pepper.
3. Add one-third cup of matzo meal to #2. As you mix the matzo meal in with the other ingredients and the consistency of the matzo meal appears to be too thick, simply add a little water.
4. Heat one-quarter cup of vegetable oil in a large frying pan.
5. Mold the mixture into individual flat pancakes and then place each pancake in the frying pan. Heat on a medium light for approximately ten minutes, or until one side turns golden brown. Then turn the pancake over to finish the cooking process.
6. Remember to serve with globs of applesauce and/or sour cream.

Today, *Hanukkah* is celebrated in many Jewish communities and households as a major holiday and it often appears to be the Jewish equivalent of Christmas. To compete with the myriad of toys children celebrating Christmas receive, gifts are now given to children on each of the eight nights of *Hanukkah*. The family will start off with a small gift and gradually build up to the eighth night of the holiday when in arrives the truly expensive and special gift that the child was wishing for. It is important to remember for your purposes that *Hanukkah* is not "just like Christmas", nor is it the Jewish answer to Christmas. And that most certainly there exists no such thing as a *Hanukkah* bush that serves as a substitute for a Christmas tree.

Families that opt to celebrate both *Hanukkah* and Christmas and who are not inter-faith families have in most cases come to this decision because they want to provide their children with the extra fun and toys they feel is associated with the celebration of Christmas. This has nothing to do with the existence of dual religious convictions. No parent ever wants to see their child left out of something that they perceive to be "good". So it has evolved that there is this need to compete with the gift giving and festive aspects of the celebration of Christmas. Please remember that the only thing that these two holidays share in common is the time of the year during which they are celebrated. Oh yes, please remember to wish your friend *A Happy (<u>not</u> Merry) Hanukkah.*

WHY ARE THE CHILDREN WEARING COSTUMES IN MARCH? IS THIS THEIR HALLOWEEN CELEBRATION?

The next Jewish holiday is *Purim*, which is celebrated to commemorate the deliverance of the Jews in Biblical times from certain destruction by the good and extremely beautiful *Queen Esther* and her faithful and trustworthy advisor *Mordecai*. A man named *Haman* had concocted an evil plot to destroy the Jews, but the plot was uncovered and all were saved. It is believed that the evil *Haman* wore a tri-colored hat (similar to what was worn by the American colonists). Out of this belief has come the tradition of baking triangular shaped cookies stuffed with fruit fillings (prune, peach, poppy seed and raspberry) known as *Hamantashen* to commemorate this holiday. You will see boxes of these cookies appear in your supermarkets just in time for *Purim* which is celebrated on Adar 15 and falls a month before the celebration of *Passover.*

The celebration of *Purim* consists of attending an evening service where the *Book of Esther* known as the *Megillah* is read aloud in the synagogue. It is from this particularly long story that the expression *"a big Megillah"* has been woven into our daily speech. How often have you heard someone say, "Simply tell me what happened, I do not want to listen to a big Megillah!" On this night the children dress up in costumes with Queen Esther and Haman and Mordecai in high attendance. The big celebration takes place at night with the onset of the holiday. This is a real fun holiday and is joyously celebrated by all Jews. During the day of *Purim* everyone goes about his or her business in a normal fashion, except of course if *Purim* should fall out on the *Sabbath.*

Mom's baking duties would never have been complete for the year if she did not prepare her famous *Hamantashen*. They were in such demand by everyone who happened to have the good fortune to be in our home during the *Purim* holiday season, that one year found Mom making several batches to ship off to the college dorm room of the boy who had taken me to my senior class prom and with whom I was still dating. He ended up sharing them with all of his non-Jewish friends in the dorm.

MOM'S HAMANTASHEN

1. The ingredients are one stick of unsalted margarine left at room temperature, one teaspoon grated orange peel, one cup of sugar, one egg, two tablespoons orange juice, two cups of sifted flour, one teaspoon baking powder, and one quarter teaspoon of salt.
2. Preheat the oven to 400 degrees.
3. Cream margarine with grated orange peel until soft and smooth. Gradually cream in sugar until the mixture is light.
4. Add the egg and the orange juice to #3 and cream and beat until the mixture becomes fluffy.
5. Sift dry ingredients together and add to #4. Blend together to make a soft dough and cover and chill in the refrigerator for several hours, or even overnight.
6. Roll on lightly floured surface until one-eighth thick in size. Cut into three-inch circles.
7. Prepare the traditional prune filling which will be placed in the center of each circle. To make the prune filling you will mix together one jar of prune lekvar, one-half cup of chopped nuts and one or two drops of lemon juice.
8. Take one teaspoon of the prepared prune filling and place in the center of each circle. Fold the circle over and pinch the circle so that it becomes triangular in shape.
9. Bake in the oven for ten minutes, or until each cookie becomes light brown in color. This recipe will yield 28 to 30 cookies.

For whatever reason, Mom would usually prepare her great corned beef and cabbage dish during the week we would be celebrating *Purim*. Certainly during my growing up years the concept of corned beef and cabbage being associated with a holiday known as St. Patrick's Day was totally alien to me. The only thing that I knew about this holiday was that it was once the answer to an extra credit question on an American history Midterm. The only thing that I knew about the Irish was that one summer I was fortunate enough to be in a High School math class being taught by a terribly funny young teacher who just happened to be Irish. He intrigued us all because he was so different from all of our Jewish teachers. In addition, he came from a part of the Bronx where a lot of non-Jews lived and where there was no need for us ever to visit, per our families! So quite honestly, whenever we would be treated to mom's great corned beef and cabbage dish during *Purim* time in March, I thought that Mom was preparing the dish to make Dad happy. After all, Dad's birthday was March 19th and this was definitely one of his favorite foods. He would always tell who ever would listen that they had never tasted real good corned beef and cabbage until they tasted his wife's dish. Prepare it and see if you agree with Dad.

MOM'S CORNED BEEF AND CABBAGE

1. The ingredients are four pounds of koshered corned beef, one five pound head of cabbage, six potatoes (preferably Red Bliss). This recipe will yield six servings.
2. Boil the corned beef in a large covered pot of water for fifteen minutes. Then pour the water out and refill the pot with cold water. Bring to a second boil and cook on a medium flame for approximately two and half-hours.
3. After the meat has cooked for two and half-hours, check with a fork for tenderness. It must be thoroughly cooked!
4. Cut the cabbage in thick enough wedges so that when the dish is ready to be served, nice thick slabs of corned beef can be prettily draped over each thick wedge of cabbage. (Mom

always taught me that presentation adds to one half of the good quality of a meal). Peel the potatoes and place them and the wedges of cabbage into the pot to cook for the last half-hour with the corned beef.

5. Serve this dish with great kosher Deli mustard!

MATZO IS A LOW FAT FOOD

Passover or *Pesach* takes place in the springtime. It will occur anytime from late March to late April It begins on Nisan 15 and is an eight-day holiday. It is my personal favorite for the way it is celebrated and for the messages and themes that are woven throughout the fiber of the holiday. The story of *Passover* is the story of the successful exodus of the Jewish people out of their bondage of slavery in Egypt and into freedom. It is said that the Jewish people fled so rapidly from the evil Egyptian tyrant, Pharaoh that they did not have the time to prepare their own food properly. In particular, they did not have the time to bake their breads properly and have them rise. Thus is born the concept of *Passover* being synonymous with unleavened bread and the eating of only matzo (unleavened bread) during the entire eight day holiday. This concept is center stage throughout the holiday and so no leaven is to be kept in the house and no leaven products are to be eaten. It is for this reason that all Orthodox and many Conservative Jews will only eat special foods that are specially prepared for *Passover* during the entire eight-day holiday. Almost everyone will have matzo and many *Passover* food products in their home.

The story of *Passover* would not be complete without an explanation of the word itself which when divided into two words stands by itself as the phrase *to pass over*. The concept of passing over refers to the last plague which God is said to have brought upon the people of Egypt for not listening to his hand picked messenger, *Moses,* who consistently begged the Egyptian leader, *Pharaoh*, to release the Hebrews from their bondage in Egypt and let them travel to the *promised land* (what is today *Israel*). The last deadly plague was the killing the first born son of each family living in Egypt.

Moses told all of the Hebrews that the Lord would be sending the *angle of death* to take the life of each first born son. To be certain that the angle of death would not take the life of any Jewish first-born male child, the community was instructed to mark their doorposts with lamb's blood. Thus, when the deadly night arrived and the *angle of death* visited each home to complete his mission, he *passed over* every home that was marked with the lamb's blood. That deadly night, according to the Bible, also took the life of the first born son of the *Pharaoh*. In rage and deep grief, *Pharaoh* summoned *Moses* to the palace and told him to tell the people of Israel to pack up whatever belongings they had and to leave Egypt immediately.

You will know that the onset of this holiday is near when you begin to see in all of your supermarkets those famous signs that read: PASSOVER FOOD SECTION. These special foods can only be prepared in pots and in pans, served on dishes, and eaten with silverware that are not used at any other time of the year. If you go back to the engagement party or wedding gift discussion portion of this book, you can now understand why I suggested the purchase of a fairly inexpensive set of dish ware or silverware for *Passover* use as an excellent gift for any young couple who is planning to observe this holiday in a traditional manner.

When you hear your friend speaking about *changing their dishes* you know that an entire kitchen is being changed and a new one is being put in place for the celebration of *Passover*. Before the *Passover* food products can be brought into the kitchen and properly put away, any foods that are in the pantry must be taken out and removed for the holiday. This also includes any and all perishable refrigerated foods. I have always tried to give away these perishable "remaining foods" to one of my none-Jewish friends or acquaintances. One year I had the pleasure and privilege to share an office and a friendship with a young man who was not Jewish. Unfortunately, like my son he met an untimely death. One of my favorite memories of him took place on the day we had attended a play performance. At the end of the day I had invited him to come inside our home in order to give him our remaining refrigerator items because we were preparing for *Passover*. Both myself and my son, who was still in elementary school, kept giving him items as he stood in the middle of our kitchen laden with food and laughing (he had the most infectious laugh) with partial gratitude and with partial disbelief at what was unfolding before his eyes. On my sons' part it had turned into a game to see how much my friend could balance and was willing to take. But he was living alone and this was a real bonanza for him! For me, whenever I savor the memories of the mosaic that made up our wonderful but all too brief friendship, I am so glad for this particular memory.

A BEAUTIFUL STORY IS TOLD

The highlight of the celebration of *Passover* are the two evening seders which are conducted at home. At each *seder* the story of *Passover* is told as everybody in attendance at the table reads a part of the story from a book known as the *Haggadah*. The reading is done either in Hebrew or in English. In our home we have established the tradition of going around the table and of having each of our guests read a paragraph in whatever way they are most comfortable doing so. Our *seder* guests run the gamut from Orthodox Jew to Reform Jew to our dear friend who is a former nun. A *Kiddush* is recited, four cups of wine are drunk, there are songs to sing, and a festive meal to be served and eaten. If at all possible, try to get yourself invited to a *seder*. I promise that you are in for a real "feel good" experience. Our close friend who had been in a convent for nine years always looks forward to joining us for one of the *seder nights*. She has told us that it brings back memories of her days in the convent when a yearly *seder* was always conducted to commemorate the last meal of Jesus Christ. One more thing! As your friend leaves to begin the holiday, be sure to call out *Have A Zeisen ("sweet") Pesach*. You can be certain that Jews of all persuasions are attending or are conducting a *seder* in different degrees of adherence to the law and to the history of the celebration of this holiday.

After spending the first few days of *Passover* enjoying brisket, turkey and chicken, we were definitely always ready for a change of pace as we sailed into the last two days of the holiday. It became a tradition in our home (due greatly to my son's urging), that I prepare my *Passover* lasagna dish which would last for two nights. Serve it with a salad with *kosher for Passover* Italian salad dressing, and one could almost imagine oneself in Rome. Or, should I say that I found myself always wishing that I were in Rome after having spent the last eight days in the kitchen. *Passover* is very much a home and kitchen holiday.

TOBY'S PASSOVER LASAGNA

1. The ingredients are six large onions (of course chopped and to this must be added a large box of tissues), three pounds of chopped meat, six eggs, one cup of white wine, one-half cup of cooking oil, eight full pieces of matzo, two cans of tomato-mushroom sauce, and a dash (?) of salt and pepper for taste.
2. Sauté the cut up onions in oil until tender. Then add the meat and cook until the redness disappears.
3. Add the tomato-mushroom sauce, the salt and pepper to #2.
4. Beat the eggs and then add the wine.
5. Line a baking pan with aluminum foil and grease the pan.
6. Using two matzos for each layer, take one matzo at a time and dip it into the egg-wine mixture (#4).
7. Add one-third of the meat mixture and place two more soaked matzos on top of the meat mixture.
8. Repeat the process described in #7, alternating the meat and matzos and topping.
9. Pour any remaining egg-wine mixture over the prepared dish.
10. Cover the aluminum foil and place in a preheated 375-degree oven for one and half-hours.

Due to the fact that observing the eight days of Passover faithfully translates into constant preparation of food and constant entertaining, one can never have or share enough recipes for *Passover*. I am fortunate enough to be able to have Mom's friend Sunny share with me two of her fantastic *Passover* recipes. She is a seasoned veteran of hosting and preparing for large groups of people in attendance at *seders* held in her home throughout the years. I hope that you will try them and find them equally fantastic!

SUNNY'S EGGPLANT AND GREEN PEPPER KIGEL

1. The ingredients are one large eggplant (should be two pounds in size when weighed together), one diced onion, one diced green pepper, salt and pepper to taste, two large eggs that have been slightly beaten, two tablespoons of butter or margarine, and one full sheet of matzo that has been crumbled.
2. Peel the eggplant and dice it into two-inch cubes. Cook the eggplant in water that has been salted and is simmering. Cook covered for approximately twenty minutes. Put a fork through the eggplant cubes to check for their tenderness. When they are tender, they are done.
3. Sauté the onion and the pepper in olive oil over a medium heat until they are tender, but not crisp. Add salt and pepper.
4. Mix the eggplant with the slightly beaten eggs and vegetable mixture and add the crumbled matzo and mix well.
5. Place the mixture in a greased baking dish and dot the top with butter or parve margarine (to allow you to serve with meat dishes). Bake in a 350-degree oven for 35 to 40 minutes, or until it has turned a golden brown.
6. This recipe makes six to eight servings.

SUNNY'S NO-BAKE SEVEN LAYER CAKE THAT CAN BE PREPARED THROUGHOUT THE YEAR

1. The ingredients are three and a half ounces of either bittersweet chocolate or milk chocolate, one quarter pound of margarine, three separated eggs, one cup of sweet wine, eight whole pieces of matzo, one-half cup of chopped walnuts, one and a half ounces of chocolate for curls and this chocolate can be either bittersweet of milk chocolate.

2. Melt the chocolate over warm water in a double boiler and allow the chocolate to cool off.
3. In a medium size bowl cream the butter of margarine with the sugar until fluffy. Add sugar and then the egg yolks, one at a time as you beat them well.
4. In a medium size bowl beat the egg white until they are stiff. Fold in the cooled off melted chocolate and also fold in the stiffly beaten egg whites.
5. Pour the sweet wine into a large shallow pan. Dip each matzo, one at a time, into the wine so that the matzo becomes moist, but not soaked.
6. Place one matzo onto a serving plate and cover with one and a half tablespoons of the chocolate filling. Top with another moistened piece of matzo and again cover with the chocolate filling. Continue this process until the eighth and final piece of matzo is on the top.
7. Cover the top and the sides with the remainder of the filling.
8. Decorate the top with chopped nuts and chocolate curls.
9. Cover the cake loosely with plastic wrap and let the cake mellow in the refrigerator for twenty-four hours.
10. Cut into small squares and serve and enjoy (**PER SUNNY**)

A CELEBRATION OF SPRING?

The last holiday to be celebrated is *Shavuot*. It is celebrated on Sivan 6, always occurring fifty days after the first day of *Passover*. In the days of the Bible, it was observed as an agricultural holiday marking the end of the barley and the beginning of the wheat harvest. During this holiday you will find that all of the synagogues are decorated with green plants. It has become customary for Orthodox Jews in particular to eat only dairy products (with the exclusion of the *Sabbath*) due to the fact that in one of our biblical books the *Torah* has been compared to milk. Conservative and Reform Jews will try to ingest a greater abundance of dairy product oriented meals than they normally would. This would be the time when Mom would treat us to her cheese blintzes and sour cream to fulfill the obligation of eating only dairy laden meals. We were always ready to enjoy them any time of the year. Try this dish and see if you agree!

MOM'S CHEESE BLINTZES

1. The ingredients are two well beaten eggs, one unbeaten egg, one cup of cold water, one cup of flour, a taste of salt (I certainly hope that you understand this form of measuring because I do not), one-half pound of farmer cheese, a teaspoon of sugar and one to two tablespoons of butter.
2. As the eggs are well beaten, gradually beat in the cold water. Beat in the flour and the salt, a little at a time.
3. Lightly grease a small frying pan or a crepe pan. Spoon in enough butter to cover the bottom of the pan and then tip the pan to all sides for a good covering, letting a lip form as the batter seems to climb up one side of the frying pan.
4. When the pancake pulls away from the sides of the frying pan and looks dry turn it out onto a dry dishtowel. Do not attempt to cook the pancake on the other side.
5. Prepare the filling by thoroughly blending the farmer cheese, the one egg and the sugar. Spoon a small amount into each pancake. Place it on the fried side. Roll the pancake up and tuck in the ends to make it appear like the side of an envelope.
6. Melt one or two tablespoons of butter in a large skillet and brown the blintzes on both sides.
7. This recipe yields fourteen individual blintzes. Serve hot with a lot of sour cream.
8. Mom's *Shavuot* blintzes were so good that she would create a nondairy version of them to serve with her meat dishes throughout the year. Simply replace the farmer cheese filling with one cup of mashed potatoes, well seasoned and mix with one-third of a cup of sautéed chopped onion. Remember to also replace the butter with *parve* margarine if you are serving *kosher*.

CHAPTER SIX: My Friend Died

One day you receive the awful and saddening news that death has touched your friend, or one of your friend's family members. Whether or not the decedent had been sick and death was somewhat expected, whether or not the decedent has died suddenly, whether or not the decedent was very young or very old or somewhere in between – the news is always shocking and never comes at the right time! As you find yourself getting caught up in the funeral preparations, it may seem to you that the swiftness and the suddenness of the act of death itself is somehow being reflected in the way in which members of the Jewish faith go about burying their dead.

NO WAKE – JUST A QUICK FUNERAL AND BURIAL

The dead are always buried within twenty-four hours of death. As with everything, there are exceptions. Traditionally the dead are not buried on the *Sabbath* or on a Festival Holy Day. If a very close family member such as a child, grandchild, spouse, parent or grandparent needs the time to travel to the funeral site, the funeral will be delayed to accommodate their travel arrangements. Finally, traditionally members of the Jewish faith prohibit an autopsy because they do believe in sacred honor of the human body. But in certain cases where a police investigation is ongoing, then the family will reluctantly agree to a limited autopsy, which will also delay the funeral arrangements.

THE FUNERAL

On the day of the funeral there will be no viewing of the body because Jewish law dictates that the casket be closed. Orthodox Jews and many Conservative Jews will bury their loved ones in a plain, pine casket. There is nothing decorative or ornate about the casket. When you are given a time for the funeral try to arrive at least a half hour in advance of that time so that you will have the opportunity to speak with the bereaved family members. They will be seated in a sort of reception room outside of the sanctuary where the ceremony will take place and where the closed casket has already been placed. The one theme that you will find running through a Jewish funeral and burial is that the death of the loved one is *God's will* and therefore the mourning should be controlled. There should be no displays of anger, rage or excessive grief.

Before the funeral service begins, the mourners have a portion of their clothing torn as a sign of mourning. The Bible speaks about the rendering of garments as a mourning custom. That torn garment is to be worn throughout the entire week while *sitting shiva*. When the time comes for the service to begin, if the family members are Orthodox, be prepared for the fact that there will again be separate seating of men and women just as there are at joyous occasions. Conservative and Reform Jews will sit together. Men will again be given the little *kipahs* or *yarmulkes* to wear, but this will be optional among Reform Jews. You will also see little round imitation lace circles with fastening pins attached to them. These are provided, in Orthodox circles, for those Jewish women who are married. They use them as make shift hats and put them on their heads before entering the sanctuary to begin the service. If you are ever present in an Orthodox synagogue you will quickly observe that a great majority of the women present are wearing hats. If they did not arrive wearing a hat, then they are provided with these circular pieces of imitation lace to use as a makeshift hat.

NO ONE SENT FLOWERS?

You will immediately notice that there are no wreaths or the standard funeral arrays of flowers. Please do not arrange for flowers to be sent to the funeral chapel or to the home. Jewish families in mourning traditionally do not want flowers. If you do want to do something in the nature of a donation, donations to a favorite charity and the planting of trees in Israel are always considered to be in good taste.

In my own case, I was the recipient of a very loving and thoughtful gesture from my dear neighbor and friend. She had brought a beautiful arrangement of red roses to our home the day before the funeral. Knowing that roses are my favorite flowers, she had wanted to do something personal to try and cheer me up. That beautiful arrangement of roses sat on our dining room table the entire week as a constant reminder of her friendship and love and concern for me. Whenever I looked at them I was also reminded of the time my son had planted two red rose bushes outside our kitchen window so that I could derive pleasure from them whenever I was involved with kitchen chores. That was a good memory and I took solace in going back to that memory throughout the entire *shiva* week.

FIRST MENTION OF THE SHIVA

The funeral ceremony is usually short with eulogies being given by the family rabbi, as well as family members and friends. At the end of the ceremony the family rabbi will give the address telling you where the family will be *sitting shiva*, as well as to what causes and existing charities the family would like any donations to be made to. The funeral ends with the pallbearers escorting the casket out of the chapel into a waiting hearse. Everyone will meet again on the grounds of the ceremony for the burial.

THE BURIAL

In the Orthodox tradition the casket is lowered manually with long ropes that have been tied around the casket. Then only family members and friends will shovel the dirt into the grave until it is filled in its entirety. Everyone remains at the burial sight until this task has been completed. Orthodox Jews feel very strongly about not having strangers (the gravediggers), who in many cases will be non-Jewish, fill in the gravesite. I can still remember the sight of my then fourteen year old son dutifully filling in the entire grave of his grandfather because he would not allow any stranger to perform this last most personal act of love and concern for "his poppy." In most Conservative and Reform burials the casket is not lowered manually and all in attendance will leave before the grave is filled in by the cemetery gravediggers. You may hear it said that "so and so" has brought with them to the cemetery dirt from the Holy Land with the express purpose of throwing it on the grave. After the burial everyone in attendance disperses quickly. The immediate family goes directly home to begin *sitting shiva* or to begin the *shiva period.*

SITTING SHIVA

Shiva is the Hebrew word for the number seven. Traditionally there is a week, or seven days of mourning. Orthodox Jews and most Conservative Jews observe this time frame. Many people, both in the Conservative and the Reform movement, have shortened the mourning period to only three days. In all cases if a Jewish holiday should happen to fall any time during the s*hiva* period, then the s*hiva period* ends immediately. The s*hiva* is always superseded by a holiday or by the onset of the *Sabbath.*

YOU DON'T HAVE TO BE JEWISH

The s*hiva period* is the time for friends and relatives to come and pay their respects and give their condolences. Let me stress the fact that the s*hiva period* is open to everyone, both Jew and non-Jew alike. It takes place both during the day and in the evening so that everyone who wants to visit can find a suitable time frame in which to do so. There is no need to call the home in advance of your arrival. The concept is one of an open house. The family members are at home in a state of mourning and all are welcome to visit at any reasonable time of the day or evening. A good rule of thumb to follow is not to arrive any earlier than 10:00 a.m., or any later than 10:00 p.m.

The only time during the entire week when there is *no sitting shiva* is with the onset of the *Sabbath.* The *Sabbath* is viewed as a happy and holy day and always takes precedence over mourning. The

Jewish religion dictates that those members of the household who are in mourning *get up from their shiva* and allow themselves the time needed to cook and prepare for the *Sabbath* meal. Therefore, the mourners will stop *sitting shiva* on Friday afternoon and resume when the *Sabbath* ends on Saturday evening.

HOW DO I ACT?

As you approach the home where the family is *sitting shiva* the most important thing to keep in mind is that this visit is not to be conducted as a regular social call. The tone is set as soon as you arrive *to pay your shiva call* and find that the front door is unlocked and that you are expected to simply walk in. After all, if you are paying a social call, you would first ring the doorbell, but this is not done when you enter a Jewish home that is in mourning. As you enter this home, you will find the mourners seated on low stools, wooden boxes, or low chairs. They are required to do so. So do not out of sympathy for them begin to insist that they take a seat on a more comfortable chair or on the couch. If a mourner happens to get up from their seat, do not sit on it. Those seats are provided only for them. The Bible describes sitting on the ground as a mourning custom and this low seat symbolizes the acting out of that custom. You will see, where at all possible, that the mirrors are covered and in most instances, the mourners are not wearing makeup, perfume and are indeed wearing the cut clothing they had on during the funeral. This is not a time for vanity or joy. It is a time for somber reflection, a time to honor the dead, a time to begin the healing and to slowly return to the reality of day to day life.

BUT JEWS ALWAYS SERVE FOOD, DON'T THEY?

In most instances, no food or drinks will be offered, but they are available in a nearby dining room or kitchen. Very often, as was our case, the family is fortunate to be surrounded by a close knit group of friends and family who are present throughout the entire *shiva week* to handle any entertaining needs. A member of this tight knit group who had never been thrown together and yet for some eerie reason seemed to almost instantaneously work in unison like some sort of kitchen <u>Radio City Rockettes </u>was of course my dear "friend/Sister Whom I Never Had" who is a former nun. I joked with her afterwards that she should surely qualify for the <u>Guinness Book of Records</u> as the first non-Jew to sit *shiva* for an entire week! Due to the fact that the mourners do not do any work, including food preparation for the entire s*hiva* (the *Sabbath* excluded), it is in good taste to bring with you selections of finger foods such as cakes, cookies, candy, fresh bread, nuts, or fruits. A bottle of wine is in good taste. A very dear and close family member, who I also consider to be a friend as well as a role model, had arranged for the most beautiful, elaborate and delicious selection of foods to be delivered to our home when we returned from the funeral. I will never forget her acts of kindness and generosity. She was one of the first people I had called with the tragic news and I lovingly and thankfully referred to her as "the general" throughout that entire awful week. Remember that if you are going into a *kosher home,* all of the food products being brought into that home must also be *kosher.* So remember to check those labels carefully if you are buying the food products anywhere other than in a *kosher* store or bakery.

WHAT SHOULD WE SEND?

If a group from work is thinking about what to do for the family who *is sitting Shiva*, you might want to arrange to send a fruit or cheese basket, or a food platter. Remember again, that if this is being sent to a *kosher home*, the food must come from either a *kosher* restaurant or store, or must bear all *kosher* food markings. The names of such establishments can easily be found in your telephone yellow pages under the listing of "*kosher*" and/or "restaurants". When I was *sitting Shiva* a large number of my co-workers arranged for enough *kosher* food to be sent to our home so that it easily could have fed all of New Jersey! The arrival to our home of such amounts of wonderfully tasting food from these equally wonderful people was both overwhelming and at the same time greatly appreciated. The day it arrived happened to be an extremely busy day of visitation for us, which culminated in an equally busy evening. In the evening very dear, life-long family friends had driven quite a distance to see us. The ability to be able to serve them such wonderful, fresh restaurant food was not lost on anyone. While they ate, we mourners were able to sit in the living room and talk with others.

WHAT DO I SAY?

And speaking of talking, you might just be asking yourself what do I say and what do I talk about when I arrive to *pay my shiva call*. The best rule of thumb is to let the family in mourning take the lead. They may still be in a state of shock, or may exhibit a great need to talk with you about the events surrounding the death of their loved one. They may also very well be able and eager to talk about the "news of the day", whether it be work or school or extra curricular activity related. Please bear in mind that your presence and concern and friendship are the greatest gifts that you can bring to these people in mourning.

THIS IS NOT A PARTY

Please bear in mind that a *shiva call* should not be planned to last all afternoon or all evening. Plan a short and respectful visit on your part. If you notice that the home is filling up quickly, stay only a half-hour. If you see that you are the only visitor and the mourners are in need of conversation, then do stay longer. Use your own common sense and good judgment and you will be fine. As you are about to leave, do not suggest that you will swing by tomorrow and take the mourner out to lunch for a change of pace and atmosphere. The mourner remains at home throughout the entire week of *shiva*. There are no luncheon or dinner breaks outside of the home.

PLEASE CALL!

Please feel free to place a telephone call to your friend during the week of mourning. In most cases a person who is not in mourning will answer the telephone, but your friend will be able to take the call. In that call you might suggest that when your friend *gets up from sitting shiva* you would like to meet for lunch or dinner. Always bear in mind that it is after the seven days of mourning when the visits stop, and time comes for the close knit band of friends and family who surrounded the mourners, to return to their own real lives, that your friend will really need some special time with you. So if you cannot pay a *shiva call* during that week that has been set aside to do so, do not despair! Know that the time you are planning to give to your friend in the days and months to come may turn out to be the most precious and needed gift of all.

THE UNVEILING

Approximately one year after death, you will hear your friend speak about the planning of an *unveiling*. This ceremony is performed to commemorate the erection of the tombstone. It is a simple ceremony conducted at graveside and most often attended by only close relatives and a few close friends. Prayers are said, in particular the prayer for the dead (*Kaddush*). At least one eulogy is given. Once again, if the decedent embraced the Orthodox ideology, you will see all of the men wearing *kipahs* and all of the married women in hats. One note of caution, please do not be offended if you simply hear of the unveiling and are not extended an invitation. Remember that this is a very short, private ceremony and that only a handful of people will be in attendance.

In the case of my son's unveiling, the ceremony did last forty minutes. Afterwards, those in attendance told me that it was by far the most beautiful and meaningful unveiling that they ever witnessed. This is in no small measure due to the way in which Rabbi Zucker conducted the unveiling. One of my son's friends spoke and addressed my son personally. My son and I had shared a love of

69

poetry and Shakespeare and during the ceremony I read the poem If by Rudyard Kipling. My son had always enjoyed hearing this poem read to him both during childhood and as an adult. As his life took on the unfortunate turns that it did, this poem took on more meaning for the both of us. I had simply wanted to read it one last time. As you can see, an unveiling can take on the tone and the ambiance of the participants. There is room for creativity in this service. One word of caution! As your friend is leaving to attend the upcoming unveiling, please do not yell out to remember to have a great time at the party!

CHAPTER SEVEN: Frequently Used Words And Phrases

There have been times during your lifetime, I am certain, when you have found yourself in either a formal or an informal setting where you have been exposed to language that is sprinkled with either "Yiddish" or "Hebrew" words and/or phrases, or as it is even sometimes referred to, "Jewish" words. How much more meaningful the conversation would have been for you if you were able to grasp the meaning of these words and phrases. When one thinks about the vocabulary and phraseology used in Jewish communities to capture the core of emotions being felt during specific lifetime experiences, you are struck by how much salt and pepper is added to the savoring and the understanding of the moment at hand when commingled with these Hebrew and Yiddish words and phrases.

Many of the most commonly used of these words and phrases I have tried to sprinkle throughout this reference book in highlighted italicized print. Many of these words and phrases have become so a part of our everyday speech that they can almost be put into the category of colloquialisms. What follows is just a smattering of such additional words and phrases with the hope that it will help to bring greater clarity and understanding the next time that you are exposed to them. I have also taken the liberty of elaborating on some of these definitions so that what follows may very well seem to you to be a little book within a little book.

Amen: It means in Hebrew, "So Be It" and is most commonly used as a response to prayer.

B'Nai Brith: It means in Hebrew "Sons of the Covenant". It is the name given to the oldest Jewish charitable organization. It attracts participants from all three ideologies.

Cantor: The Hebrew word is *Hazzan.* This is the person who is in charge of the synagogue music. The cantor will also lead the congregation in prayer and does play a very big role on *Yom Kippur.* For it is the cantor who sings the beautiful melodic *Kol Nidre* as the sun sets and the Jewish community prepares to usher in the Day of

Atonement with fasting and prayer. This is such a special role and time that very often a congregation who cannot afford to hire a cantor for its all year round services will arrange to have a cantor on the premises beginning with the celebration of *Rosh Hashanah* and ending with the blowing of the *shofar* at the end of the concluding service for *Yom Kippur*.

Chutzpah: It is a Yiddish word and it means the display of an almost sarcastic indifference. It can be used in the following context, "Did you know that he brought his new girl friend to his wife's funeral – what *chutzpah*!"

Chatzkas: It is a Yiddish word. It refers to a collection of items of insignificant material worth. It can be used in the following context: "I keep those little *chatzkas* on my desk at work."

Chazir: It is the Hebrew word for pig. It is used when describing the excessive behavior of someone, especially where eating habits are involved. It can be used in the following context: "Sam, I do not want you to eat that third sandwich – stop being such a *chazir*!" Or, you might hear someone making the following observation while attending a function of some sort: "What a *chazir* he is. Did you see him eating nonstop at the cocktail hour, and off of both your plate and mine."

Daven: It means to pray. The first time you might hear this word being used is in the context of a discussion concerning the time of arrival for a *Bar* or *Bat Mitzvah* service. The conversation might begin as follows, "The *davening* for the day will begin at 9:00 a.m., but it is perfectly all right if you plan to arrive at 10:00 a.m."

You may also hear the word being used in the context of an Orthodox Jewish man giving the reason for being late to work on a given morning. He may explain that the morning's *davening* took a little longer than usual.

Draydel: It is a word that describes both an item and a game that is synonymous with the celebration of *Hanukkah*. It is a Yiddish word and means "Spinning Top". A *draydel* can be made out of any material, with wood being the most traditional. Each side of the *draydel* contains a Hebrew letter which stands for the first letter of the Hebrew sentence, "A great miracle happened there." You take turns spinning the *draydel*. When I was a child, we would play for pennies.

Two or three of us would take turns at spinning the *draydel* and the one whose spin landed on the highest letter in the Hebrew alphabet would win the grand prize of a penny. You might hear someone using the word in the following manner, "My children *played draydel* each of the eight nights of *Hanukkah.*"

Erez Israel: These Hebrew words mean "the land of Israel." Often you will hear the term used by the political leaders of Israel when they appear on the Sunday morning talk shows.

Eruv: It is the Hebrew word for missing. What it translates into in modern terms is the putting in place of some sort of symbolic fencing around the perimeter of an Orthodox community. Remembering that the act of carrying is only allowed in one's home on the *Sabbath* and holidays, this allows for such acts as the carrying of a book to the synagogue, the wheeling of a baby carriage and the use of an umbrella. *Eruvs* have been set up in many communities in America and in Israel. Recently, there was a reported controversy in a suburban community in New Jersey over the establishment of an *eruv*. In particular, the debate raged over how the electrical wiring already in place in the town was being disturbed by the attempt of the Orthodox Jewish community to put the *eruv* in place.

Frum: An extremely observant Jew.

Goy: It is the Yiddish word for a gentile or a non-Jew. You may have heard of the term *Shabbas Goy*. A gentile becomes a *Shabbas Goy* when you have been asked and do consent to perform certain tasks on the *Sabbath* from which orthodox Jews are prohibited from performing. This mainly deals with turning on and shutting off the lights throughout the home. With the advent of timers there is almost no need anymore to seek out a gentile for this situation. Sometimes a person was paid to be a *Shabbas Goy* and most of the time they were not. In fact, some of you may be reading this and now are starting to think back on a time long ago when that nice Jewish woman who lived down the street would ask you to come into her home on a Saturday afternoon to boil water for her tea, or to walk her dog. If you have such a memory, then you were once a *Shabbas Goy*. Many years ago, a colleague of mine revealed to me that he had worked his way through law school by acting as a *Shabbas Goy* for the many members of an Orthodox Jewish community near Chicago.

Goyim: It is the Yiddish word for gentiles or for non-Jews.

Grace Before Meals: (Yes, the Jews have this too) This was referred to earlier in this book when dealing with the benediction said over the bread before you can begin eating. The benediction whether you are dining in an Orthodox, a Conservative or a Reform home will be said in Hebrew. It translates into: *Blessed art thou Lord God, King of the Universe, who brings forth bread from the earth.* Both followers of the Orthodox, as well as the Conservative ideology of Judaism will add a *grace after meals.* It is a benediction said after eating and is normally made up of four blessings. Children who attend Hebrew Day Schools are taught, from the earliest grades on upward to sing the grace to an upbeat melody consisting of several minutes of memorized Hebrew words.

This brings to mind a story revolving around the celebration of my son's eleventh birthday. Due to the fact that on that particular year, my son's birthday would be falling squarely in the middle of all of the Jewish holidays, the decision was made to celebrate with a swim party on a late hot August afternoon. A group of rambucious eleven-year-old boys and myself spent the afternoon at our development swimming pool. A young woman who was not Jewish and who I had just shared an office with for several months, agreed to join us at the pool and volunteered to also pick up the birthday cake for us. After swimming, we went back home for food and the birthday cake. The entire group of young partygoers had been enjoying an aggressively loud, good time in the pool and it carried through during dinner and the cake eating and food throwing festivities which followed. Upon finishing eating, just as if a switch had somehow been magically turned off, this boisterous group turned into a group of angelic looking "choir boys" as they dutifully and joyously began to sing their grace after meals in Hebrew and without any books to guide them. I will never forget the look of astonishment on the face of this guest as she witnessed and heard the instantaneous transformation that took place in our dining room that hot August day so many years ago.

Hasid: It means "pious one". A person who is a member of the *Hassidic* movement.

Hasidim: The Hebrew word for "the pious". This 18th century movement elevated individual piety to a status even higher than scholarship in the *Torah*.

This group of Jews tends to set themselves apart from secular society and, indeed, even from their fellow Jews who adhere to Conservative and Reform ideologies. The most obvious way in which they differ is their extremely modest way of dressing. You will most often, regardless of the season of the year, see the men and boys dressed in very conservative dark black slacks, suits and long sleeve white shirts. They wear dark colored ties. You will never see the young boys and male teenagers wearing the trendy fashions of the day. If you happen to live near such a community, you will notice that when the men and teenage boys walk to *Sabbath* services, they wear large brimmed black hats. From this has come the slang expression of referring to this group of Jews as "the black hats." Women and young girls as well are required to dress extremely modesty, which translates into covering the entire body. Therefore, it can be the hottest day of the summer and you will notice them wearing long sleeve blouses and long skirts. The standard male dress code has led to many a person mistaking a member of this sect for a member of the Amish community. But unlike the Amish, the Hasidim will use electricity, and own an automobile. This of course applies to any time when it is not a *Sabbath* or a holiday.

Their observance of the letter of the law is so strict that they have even set up their own community services within the confines of their restricted and close-knit communities. They send their children to their own schools where the emphasis is heavily on the study of *Torah*. This includes the high school years. It is very rare that members of this group allow their children to attend college, nor do they co-mingle with anyone who is attending secular schooling. Their childhood is very different from that of other American boys and girls. I have only had one occasion to be in the home of such a family with small children. What struck me is that there was no television, no radio and no toys for the children to play with. This particular family lived so close to FAO Schwartz– but oh so far! People who embrace this ideology truly believe that the best is yet to come when we pass from this world to the next. Hence, there is no emphasis on appearance, on worldly possessions. This includes furnishings and all of the things that we all get caught up in making certain that our children have and are exposed to.

It should not surprise you to learn that arranged marriages are still carried out among the *Hasidim*. Indeed, the marriage ceremony itself is held outside so that the young couple can be married underneath the stars. If you live close to such a community, it is not an odd occurrence to find yourself walking home from work one evening and having to pass through an ongoing wedding ceremony being conducted in the middle of the street.

The *Hasidim* will only buy and eat *kosher meat* that has been prepared in such a way as to considered *Glatt Kosher*. This means that the meat has gone through the koshering process, and then an additional effort is made to drain as much blood out of the meat as is possible.

Keep in mind that as a group they are very insular. They do not want to assimilate into society, Israeli society included. A great example of this concerns bus transportation. Spring Valley, New York has a large *Hassidic* community. Many of the men need to commute to New York City each day. Many work in the famous New York City jewelry district. These commuters board a bus each morning that has been especially equipped for them to say their morning prayers (*daven*). The bus contains an altar, a *Torah*, and prayer books. So do not think that your eyes are playing tricks on you if you one-day find yourself on the New York Thruway next to this bus.

If you do find yourself invited to a joyous occasion, automatically know that the concept of separate permeates their lives. You will never see a married couple strolling down the street holding hands! You should also know that if you do receive an invitation to a wedding or to a Bar Mitzvah, consider yourself quite honored since it is very rare for the *Hasidim* to interact with people who do not follow their way of life.

Hatikvah: It is the title of the national anthem of Israel. It is the Hebrew word for <u>hope</u>. You may at some time find yourself invited to attend a gathering being sponsored by a Jewish organization. After the singing of our national anthem, you will hear the beautiful melodic melody, based on a Sephardic melody, begin to be played and you will no doubt be surprised as you look around the room and see how many of your All-American friends and colleagues know and sing the words to the *Hatikvah* as well as they do the words to the <u>Star Spangled Banner</u>.

Hebrew: It is the language of the ancient Israelites. It was chosen as the official language of the State of Israel when statehood was declared in Mary 1948.

High Holy Days: The ten-day period that begins with the observance of *Rosh Hashanah* and concludes with the observance of *Yom Kippur*.

Jerusalem: It is the capital city of Israel. The issue of whether or not Jerusalem should become a divided city and thus in the hands of the religious groups to whom it is a sacred and holy city (Christians, Muslims and Jews) continues to tear apart the Middle Eastern Region of the world and to stand as a major obstacle on the road to real peace in this part of the world. I will never be able to separate my thoughts of this city from how I experienced the sight of it for the first time. It was late in the afternoon on a very hot Sunday in August 1985. It was at a time when it was still considered safe to tour areas that are unfortunately no longer safe havens. We were driving to this beautiful city with my husbands' cousin who was and still is the mayor of the Upper Galilee region. He and his wife had accompanied us on a wonderful three-day tour, which ended with this crowning jewel of a city – Jerusalem. Both men had fought in the 1967 and the 1973 wars. As our car wound up into the hills leading to this majestic city (it truly is God's city), the streets and buildings began to come into focus. Suddenly these two men, both quiet and reserved by nature, burst into song. They were singing the song that had become the victory song of the 1967 war: *Jerusalem of Gold*. The song has poignant music to accompany its stirring lyrics. The way in which this song accompanied us into Jerusalem ripped through my heart as I saw for the first time the city that so many had fought and died over and are still fighting and dying over as I am writing this.

L'Shanah Tovah: It is the Hebrew phrase for Happy New Year. You will often see it printed on Jewish New Year cards. Try saying it to your friends as they take leave to begin the observance of *Rosh Hashanah*. The expressions on their faces will be well worth your efforts.

Kibbitz: To joke or fool around.

Kibbitzer: A person who enjoys joking or fooling around.

Kibbutz: An Israeli agricultural collective. One of the unique facets of life on a kibbutz is that the children are separated and live apart from their parents at a very early age. This idea was initially conceived in order to allow the women members of the *kibbutz* the freedom to attend to all of their responsibilities. The parents do visit with their children throughout the day and as the years have past, many *kibbutzes* allow the families to stay intact. I visited a *kibbutz* for one day and what stood out in my mind was what I saw on the outskirts of the community. There could be seen the remnants of entire Arab planes that the members of this *kibbutz* had shot out of the sky during an air attack on their little village during the 1948 war with the Arab nations which broke out the same day that Israel became an independent country! Having visited Williamsburg, Virginia a few years earlier, I felt that what I saw in Israel that day gave new meaning to the famous advertisement for Williamsburg, Virginia: "That the present may learn from the past."

Kvetch: To complain. Someone who complains is a *kvetch*. A parent may often use this word in the following context: "Stop being such a *kvetch* and take out the garbage."

Mashuganah: It is the Yiddish word for someone who is acting or talking as if they are crazy.

Mench: It is the Yiddish word for an exceptionally good and decent person. The word can be used in the following context: "He is always using his position to do good deeds for others and always goes about it in such a quiet and modest manner. What a *mench* he is."

This word is also part of a popular Yiddish expression, which translated into English is "the *mench* (a person) plans, and God laughs".

Mezuzah: It is the Hebrew word for doorpost. A *mezuzah* consists of a parchment scroll that is placed in a small container and then is attached at an angle to the right side of each door post in a Jewish home, beginning with the front door and continuing throughout the home to every entrance to what is deemed to be a room. The words contained on the parchment paper fulfill the obligation of every Jewish family to write God's words upon the doorposts of their houses. This is how a Jewish home is distinguishable from that of a non-Jewish home. This of course always reminds me of the famous *Passover* story that instructed the Hebrews who were in bondage in Egypt to mark their doorposts with lamb's blood. Today, a great market has grown up around the production of beautiful *mezuzah* cases. These cases can range in price from inexpensive to costly art works created by prominent Israeli artists and sold at a price of upwards of $900. Lenox makes a very nice *mezuzah* case and that has always been my choice. All Orthodox and most Conservative homes will have *mezuzahs* on their front doors as well as throughout the home. Many Reform homes will have at least an outside *mezuzah*.

Mikveh: It is a ritual bath that is used for ritual cleansing for women a week after the completion of their menstrual cycle. Women who are converting to Judaism are also expected to go to the *mikveh* as an intregal part of a woman's conversion to Judaism. Many religious women go to the *mikveh* each Friday afternoon, before the onset of the Sabbath, and most definitely before their wedding day. The connotation of purity is associated with the act of fully submerging oneself in the *mikveh*.

I have only been to a *mikveh* once. It was on the Friday afternoon before I married for the first time at the young age of twenty-two. I was quite apprehensive about the experience and my mother actually went with me. We walked to an unfamiliar neighborhood in the Bronx and entered a small brick building attached to a synagogue. I was escorted to a small room and told to get totally undressed. I then entered another room which contained a small pool that resembled a standard sized kiddy pool. I was then told to get into the pool, walk to the middle of the pool and totally submerge myself so that I could feel the water going through every part of my body. An older woman who bore an uncanny resemblance to my eighth grade gym teacher, sat on a chair near the edge of the pool and recited a blessing in Hebrew for each of the three times that I was asked to submerge myself. As I left the pool area and began to quickly dress, I remember thinking that if I was able to survive this experience; I am ready for anything that my new life may bring. How foolishly optimistic! Apologies in advance if what I am about to reveal might seem to border on the irreverent, but my father had a wonderful sense of humor. Whenever the topic of dream jobs would come up, my father would always say that he would love to have the opportunity to work as a lifeguard in a *mikveh*.

Minyan: The ten adult men (any male over the age of thirteen) that are required to make up the quorum for communal prayer. This is a firm and fast rule in all Orthodox synagogues. Today, at all Conservative and Reform synagogue services, women are counted as part of the *minyan* needed to begin the prayer service.

Mitzvah: A divine commandment derived from the *Torah*. It is used to refer to the doing of a good deed. The word can be used in the following context: "What a *mitzvah* I performed today. I brought food and medicine to my elderly, sick grandmother."

Nachas: It is the Hebrew word for joy. It is most commonly used to convey to others the joy that a particular loved one gives you. You will often here it used in the following context, upon the birth of the baby: "May he or she always be a great source of *nachas* to you."

Noodge: A person who is acting in a mildly annoying way. The act of being mildly annoying. A parent might say to their child: "Please stop whining and clinging to me. Stop being such a *noodge* and go upstairs and begin your homework.

Oy Vey: It is Hebrew for Oh No. It is often uttered during a moment of mild frustration such as when a parent is heard to say: "*Oy Vey*! He threw his shoes in the toilet bowl again!"

Sanctuary: it is the room found in the synagogue where Jewish worship takes place. It is the room you will be siting in as you witness the unfolding of a Jewish marriage ceremony.

Sephardim: It means Jews of Spanish origin. In modern day American and Israeli terms the word is used to refer to those Jews who are not considered to be Askenzaim. The Sephardim are those Jews who can trace their ancestry back to Spain before the Spanish rulers handed down an edict in 1492 to expel all Jews from their country. Herein lies the fuel for the centuries long speculation that Christopher Columbus might have been a Jew who was seeking a way to flee from a homeland where he and his people were no longer wanted. After 1492 the Jews who had lived in Spain found refuge in the North African countries, in Italy, in the Ottoman Empire and subsequently found their way to the New World. One of the oldest synagogues in the United States is The Sephardic Synagogue located in New York City. Having married into a Sephardic family, it has been my pleasure over the years to be treated to some wonderful family dishes. My particular favorite features couscous as the star and main ingredient. Couscous is very popular in Morocco, Algeria, Tunisia and Libya, which are all countries located in Northern Africa. Couscous grains are steamed in a double boiler known as a Couscousier over a stew of either lamb, chicken, or meat and vegetables. In Tunisia and Libya cooked fish is used instead of the lamb, chicken or beef. What follows is one of my sister-in-law's great recipes for:

COUSCOUS WITH LAMB

The ingredients for the couscous are to simply purchase 2 to 3 boxes of plain couscous and follow the directions found on the box.

The ingredients for the lamb stew are two pounds of boneless stewing lamb, one cup of chickpeas that must be soaked at least an hour, two quarts of water, one large onion cut into quarters, two cloves of garlic which are roughly chopped, one half small head of white cabbage cut into big chunks, one turnip cut into chunks, a one half pound pumpkin cut into big chunks, a one half small zucchini which is cut in half lengthwise, one half teaspoon of paprika, one half teaspoon of turmeric, one quarter teaspoon of powdered ginger, salt and pepper.

1. Place the meat and chickpeas into a large pot or in the bottom of a cousousier. Cover with two quarts of water and bring to a boil and skim off any foam that may appear on the surface. Lower the heat and add the onion, garlic, and spices. Simmer for one hour and then add salt to taste.
2. Add to the cooking pot the carrots, cabbage, and potatoes and simmer for twenty minutes. If necessary, add more water.

3. Meanwhile, prepare the couscous. Follow the instructions on the box. When it has been prepared, place the couscous between the palms to prevent them from sticking together and forming lumps.

4. Add the turnip to the stew. Place the couscous I a steamer or a metal colander, set it inside the stew pot, cover and steam. The couscous will absorb some of the stew's fragrance. If you have decided to use a couscousier, put the couscous in the top part of the couscousier and cover. When the steam begins to rise from the couscous, it is done.

5. Ten minutes after adding the turnip add the pumpkin, zucchini and tomato and cook for another five minutes.

6. To serve, place the couscous on a large platter, tossing with a fork in order to separate the grains. Form the couscous into a mound. Make a large indentation in the center of the mound and place the meat inside. Arrange the vegetables around the couscous and pour the broth into a separate bowl.

7. Serve at once. This recipe will yield eight to ten servings.

Shalom: It is a Hebrew word that has three different meanings. It means hello, it means goodbye, and it also means peace. Jews very often greet one another this way. Jews are most certainly always hoping and praying for it to break out in the Middle East.

Shul: It is the Yiddish word for synagogue.

Simcha: It means a joyous Jewish event. The word will always be used in the context of referring to the upcoming wedding, the upcoming *Bris*, the upcoming *Bar Mitzvah,* the upcoming *Bas Mitzvah,* the upcoming birthday party, the upcoming graduation party and the upcoming anniversary party. I am not certain if it can be used in the context of a retirement party but try it and see what type of response you get!

Synagogue: It is the house of Jewish worship. Orthodox and Conservative Jews use this word when referring to their houses of worship. Reform Jews call their house of worship a *Temple*.

Rabbi: An extremely well educated person as well as a well-versed person in all aspects of Jewish law and life. A *rabbi* has received ordination. A *rabbi* is a graduate of a rabbinical seminary and different ones exist for all three Jewish ideologies. Once asked to become the spiritual leader of a particular synagogue, the duties of a *rabbi* will include officiating at all synagogue services, becoming the principal of the Hebrew school that is run on Sundays and during the week for children of the members of the synagogue. It should be strongly noted that only men are allowed to be ordained as Orthodox *rabbis* while both conservative and Reform houses of worship have women *rabbis*. Rabbis are allowed to marry. It should also be noted that the membership of the synagogue would often provide a home for the rabbi and his family. This is especially true if the community is Orthodox and located in a suburban setting. It is very important to insure that the rabbi will have housing within a reasonable walking distance from the synagogue. Remember, in all Orthodox communities one always walks to attend *Sabbath* services and holiday services and this must be done in all sorts of weather. One is not permitted to carry anything, and that includes an umbrella! Acts of carrying are only permissible when an *eruv* (see definition above) has been put in place.

Tefillin: They are also known as phylacteries. These are square leather boxes containing Scripture verses, which are to be worn around the forehead and left arm of a Jewish male over the age of thirteen. Devout Orthodox men, as well as many Conservative men, wear them during prayer each morning. The process usually takes about forty-five minutes. Thus, one must add on forty-five minutes to the usual morning preparation time needed before the workday begins. This ritual must always take place in the morning before breakfast. If one should happen to be running late, the morning *davening* cannot be made up during a lunch hour. Add to this the fact that there are certain times of the month, such as the beginning of a new month, when the *davening* takes longer than usual. It may not be uncommon to hear your Orthodox Jewish colleague explain that he was late getting into work on that particular day because he had a longer *davening*. It is rare that Jewish men who follow the Reform ideology will *daven* with *tefillin*.

Twelve Tribes of Israel: I decided to include this because I know that many of you have heard a Jew referred to, or refer to him or herself as *a member of the tribe*. These twelve tribes refer to the traditional division of the people of Israel. The Bible tells us that each tribe was descended from one of the sons of Jacob. For those of you have been treated to a production of the play by Andrew Lloyd Webber, <u>Joseph And His Amazing Technicolor Dream Coat</u>, you heard the name of each of the tribes ticked off as each son's names is called out in one of the introductory songs in the play. Ten of the tribes became lost and over the centuries speculation has sprung up over who and where the lost tribes are. There is heavy speculation that members of many American Indian tribes may actually be descendants of one or more of these lost tribes. Studies have been conducted and documented showing how the roots of many words found in the American Indian dialects can be easily be traced to Hebrew. Today the only two tribes that remain are *Levi* and *Cohen.*

Yahrzeit: It is the anniversary of the death of a close family member. It is always commemorated on the date of death as it occurs on the Jewish calendar. It is customarily observed by lighting a candle on the evening of the onset of the anniversary date. The candle burns for the next twenty-four hours. In today's modern society, we have what are known as *yahrzeit lights*, which are electric candles. You may very well hear a co-worker say: "This is not a good day for me because it is my father's *yahrzeit.*"

Yiddish: It is the language of the Askenazic Jewish community. It is written using Hebrew letters. Jewish immigrants who came to this country from Poland, Russia and Germany only spoke Yiddish. My parents spoke Yiddish to one another but a great effort was made to never speak Yiddish to and in the presence of the children. This rule was of course broken whenever they did not want us to know what they were talking about.

I had a great aunt and great uncle who looked upon me as the grandchild they never had. My great aunt could not speak a word of English. Yet somehow, I can remember always being able to speak to her in English, have her lovingly answer me in Yiddish and then I would answer her in English. So on and on would go our conversations through all the years of her life. Through my loving relationship with this aunt I learned at an early age that the barrier between two people is never about the different languages they may speak, nor the different backgrounds that they may hail from. Rather, unfortunately, such barriers are built when there exists a lack of desire and love to bridge such small obstacles and for whatever reason, an equally burning desire to make language and different backgrounds the great barrier between two people. How great become the loss, the isolation and the lack of growth.

The turn of the twentieth century gave birth to the phenomenon known as the *Yiddish Theater*. In any city that boasted a large group of recent Jewish immigrants who spoke *Yiddish,* clusters of such theaters sprung up presenting plays using only *Yiddish* dialogue and only *Yiddish* lyrics to songs. Many an actor crossed over from the world of the Yiddish Theater to Broadway. Molly Picon, the well-known actress, made such a transition. She was still going strong when while in high school I saw her perform on Broadway in the play *Milk and Honey*.

Every family is privy to the famous story, told no doubt countless times, of how Dad got Mom to marry him. My parents would probably never have married if my father had not been a musician, sang very well and had a great repertoire of *Yiddish* songs. The story goes that Mom hesitated to marry Dad because she did not know if he would be able to settle down and be a faithful husband. Dad at the time was tall, dark, extremely handsome, and had dated every woman in the department store that they both worked in, before asking my mother out on a date.

That first summer that my parents knew one another my mother went off for a one-week vacation with her girlfriends. Dad knew that my mother had a very sick mother who was recuperating from a recent heart attack. Each night my father would come over to the apartment building where my grandmother lived in a ground floor apartment, place a chair underneath her window, and serenade her with *Yiddish* songs all evening. When my mother returned from her vacation, my grandmother told her to marry my father and she did! For those of you who are now curious as to how the marriage turned out, I can only report that when their truly beautiful love affair of forty-seven and a half years ended with my father's death, we received a most beautiful letter from a cousin. In the letter she thanked my father for serving as the model in our family for how a husband and father should act.

Yiddishkeit: Jewish observance or Jewish lifestyle.

Zaddik: It is the Hebrew word for a righteous man. When attempting to describe a person who is exceptionally good and bright, who everyone goes to for counsel and advise, and who truly does God's work while here on earth, this presents the perfect opportunity to say; "He is a real *Zaddik*!"

EPILOGUE

"Much of the vitality in a friendship lies in the honoring of differences, not simply in the enjoyment of similarities."

—James L. Fredericks in
Journal of Ecumenical Studies

ABOUT THE AUTHOR

Toby R. Serrouya was born and raised in the Bronx, New York. She is a graduate of Queens College of the City University of New York. After college she moved to New Jersey to begin her professional odyssey. She taught elementary school for a number of years. She is currently working as a paralegal in the Tax Department of a New Jersey law firm. She had one son who died in the year 2000. After his death she had to battle her way back to living life again. Writing this book became a part of her therapy. She resides in Hackettstown, New Jersey with her husband, Elyse, and their cat, Menachem.